The MOTHERLAND COOKBOOK

105 African Recipes & More

THE MOTHERLAND COOKBOOK

Editor/Proof Readers
Nancy C. Fiator
Nams Nasah-Lima
Sandra Jules-Sendze

Cover Design
Jordan Fremgen
www.eyeoftheriver.com

Composition
Jordan Fremgen

Food Pictures
Phillip Smith

Printed in the United States of America
First Printing, 2014
ISBN: 978-1-4951-2001-5

Motherland Spices
3915 Andrew Jackson way
Hermitage, TN 37076

www.motherlandspices.com

TABLE OF CONTENTS

SOUPS

STEWS

VEGETABLES

ACKNOWLEDGMENTS

My customers at Motherland Kitchen were not only intrigued by the flavors but also by the variety of dishes that we served. We used the same vegetables, grains, and meats as other restaurants, but our dishes looked and tasted completely different. Since our customers continuously asked for recipes, I decided to write a cookbook that would provide them with measurements and steps that have been tested. I have also simplified the methods to make it easier for a non-traditional cook of African foods. A hearty thank you to all my customers and supporters.

To my beloved mother, Mama Anasthasia Wirba Kehla (RIP), fondly called Mam-myDoro, thank you for teaching me how to cook and share my food with others. I hope I make you proud by sharing not only the food I cook but also my methods and your cooking tips with those who want to learn.

To my daughter, Sandra Berrie Jules-Sendze, thank you for being my rock. I have completely depended upon you to achieve my goals. I cannot ask for a better daughter than you—a daughter who is not only focused but a great manager as well.

To my son-in-law, Michael Njilah Sendze, thank you for your moral and technical support. Without the original website, Motherland Spices would not have gained the national exposure it now has. I thank God for bringing you into my family.

To my brother, Zachary Kongnso Kehla and your beautiful wife, Nicole, thank you for supporting me during this process.

To my niece, Louise Asheri Nchanji, thank you for your hard work and dedication in identifying the specialty items and the authentic African herbs and spices that we use for our seasoning blends at Motherland Spices. You are the backbone of this project.

To my sisters, Mary Yengeh Njoka and Emma Yenla-Elame, thank you for igniting my desire to follow my dream and for supporting me all these years.

To my nephew, Cajetan Kehla, thank you for taking your time to analyze the recipes and give suggestions on how to make them better.

To my brother, Michel Fiator, thank you for your support and encouragement to follow my passion and dreams. They really do come true.

To my niece, Nancy C. Fiator, who diligently edited this work. Your support in this project is invaluable and I cannot thank you enough.

To my sister, Gladys Lamkum-Achiri, thank you and the girls for trying out the recipes and giving me feedback.

To my sister, Mercy Egbe Azumbi, thank you for sharing your recipes with me and for your constant support during this period.

To my sister, Comfort Tafon Uduojie, thank you for the ideas and support with the seasonings at Motherland Kitchen restaurant.

To Nana Odile Nyonga-Mullaya, thank you for all the cooking tips you gave me throughout this process.

To my aunt, Mami Martha Feh Ngwa (RIP), thank you for instilling in me the love of cooking by letting me help out when you made those delicious dishes for weddings.

To my aunt, Mami Bodzemo, thank you for the cooking tips you gave me. With your help, I have made several traditional dishes more palatable to non-Africans.

To Collette Chinje-Musa "Missneh," my special sister, thank you for helping me get the project off the ground and for encouraging me to turn my dreams into reality.

To Nams Nasah-Lima, your literary input in this project is invaluable. Thank you for taking your time to edit the work and for being a wonderful small sister.

To Yvonne Shyntum-Ebai, thank you for being a resourceful little sister, for trusting in my culinary gifts, and for being a cheerful sampler of the dishes.

To Maria Ngaibe-Bongfen, thank you and your husband, Eugene, for believing in the seasonings from the get-go and for sampling and promoting them.

To Theresa Atanga Wansi, thank you for supporting this project from the very beginning.

To my friends Lucie Ngongbo, Angeline Banobe-Doe, Flora Lamlenn, and Shira Chinje-Noumbissie, thank you all for sharing your cooking tips with me and for always taking your time to discuss and suggest other ways of making various dishes more palatable.

To my friends Hilda-Stella Ewi-Asongwe, Pamela Kisob, Mafeu Liz Mbayu, Mafor Edwan Nana Fon, Therese Mfonfu-Fomunung, Susan Bamuh-Apara, and Awazele Fossung, thank you for all the moral support and encouragement throughout this project.

To Lolem Ngong, thank you for believing in my cooking and giving me a cookbook stand that would act as a constant reminder to me to write a cookbook.

To Clay Coulter, my friend and colleague at HP Enterprise Services, Nashville, TN, thank you for helping me come up with the cookbook title and for your support with this project.

To Cortez Lee, my friend and colleague at HP Enterprise Services, Nashville, TN, thank you supporting me throughout this project and for sampling the dishes from the different recipes in this book.

To Morgan Standard, my friend and colleague at HP Enterprise Services, Nashville, TN, thank you for inspiring me to develop gluten free recipes for this cookbook.

To all my friends in the Breakfast Club at HP Enterprise Services, Nashville, TN, thank you for your support and encouragement.

THE MOTHERLAND COOKBOOK

The methods shown in this book are those that I have tested at the Motherland Kitchen restaurant. They could deviate slightly or to a great extent from the traditional methods, either because the traditional method will require an acquired taste to appreciate the dish or because I have consciously decided to change the method in other to make the final dish appealing to non-traditional palates. The change will mostly be in adding seasonings and seasoning blends.

My wish for those who buy this cookbook is that they enjoy cooking their own food and eating what they cook. It may not be perfect the first time, but with practice, it should get better. I have deliberately left out the usual "prep time, total time" metrics. Do not worry about the total time it takes. Just make up your mind to cook and enjoy the dish, no matter how long it takes. It is worthwhile to cook what you eat and enjoy what you cook. For mothers, this is an opportunity to bond with your children. Teaching your children how to cook will become very handy when they go off and live by themselves.

A Message From Sabina

"Food is your body's medicine. Cook what you eat and enjoy what you cook. That is how you guarantee the quality of what you feed your body. You keep yourself and your family happy and healthy when they eat not only healthy but tasty food that is also cost effective. There is no excuse not to enjoy your food when Motherland Spices is just a click away. We guarantee your food will taste right. If it does not come out right the first time, try again."

- Enjoy your meals
- Bon Appétit
- Buen Apetito
- Buon Appetito

– Sabina Leyla Jules

DEDICATION

To my beloved grandsons...

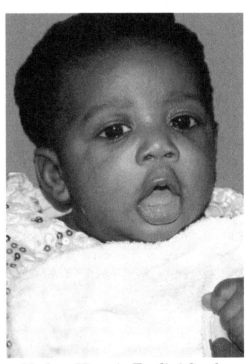

Luke Kidze Sendze   *Nathan Viserviy Tardini Sendze*

*"In life always follow your passion and strive to achieve your dreams,
for they do come true"*

GRANDMA

PREFACE

From humble beginnings, I grew up in the city of Bamenda, capital of the North Western Region of Cameroon. My parents handed down the tenets of survival—by any means decent and necessary—to me and my siblings very early on. These survival strategies that I learned were responsible for making me a passionate person.

My father died when I was very young. All upbringing duties were therefore deferred to my mother, left with six children to feed, clothe, shelter, and educate. "Mammy," as we lovingly called her, was a great cook, and logic dictated that she uses that culinary gift and passion to generate an income to make ends meet.

Mammy was not always in the best of health, so I frequently assisted her in the kitchen. In doing so, I learned much about cooking, which put me light years ahead of my peers. At the tender age of ten, I was already cooking dinner for the family on days when Mammy's asthma would flare up and she could not withstand the wood smoke or dust generated by blowing on the three-stone firewood cooking flame. Watching Mammy strain and toil for us, year in and year out, propelled me to start my own cooking business to supplement our income my high school fees.

Every summer I would operate what was called the "Dodo School." "Dodo" is the common name for fried yellow plantains. I served it with stewed beans and fried fish. With help from my mother, I quickly became familiar with different types of herbs and vegetables, especially leeks, which were used to enhance the flavor of foods. I also experimented with basil, thyme, celery, ginger, garlic, white and black pepper, and other indigenous herbs and spices.

My love for cooking has grown with age. I immigrated to the United States of America in 1984. After graduating from Kean College of New Jersey, with a degree in Computer Science, I sought employment with several Fortune 500 companies in the field of Database Administration. To keep my passion for cooking burning, I now cook for my colleagues every time the opportunity arises. At every job, my friends wonder why I bother sitting behind a computer doing a boring job when I could be having fun doing what I love—cooking. I tried it out by taking time off from the world of computing and opening a restaurant called "Motherland Kitchen" in Atlanta, Georgia, which I operated for three years. After this challenging venture, I returned to work full-time as a Database Administrator. I look back with gratitude and satisfaction for what I have achieved, in terms of introducing African Cuisine to the greater non-African population. I also came out of this venture with a lot of experiences, a few of which have led me to writing this cookbook.

While interacting with my customers, I realized that there was a need for a formal introduction of the African cuisine. The world is now a global village. Barriers of communication have been broken down by the new age of electronics, as well as the ease of travel. There are several reasons why I decided to write this cookbook.

1. Mixed marriages are more commonplace today, and there is a need for different ethnic foods in homes where one parent is of African descent and the other is either of European, Asian, American, or Caribbean descent. In-laws who typically visit teach or show how the various African dishes are made; however, when they leave, their daughters-in-law still cannot make the dishes. This is because in Africa we generally cook every dish by eyeballing the ingredients, and 99 percent of the time it comes out right. These new "citizens" of Africa need help with measurements and seasoning blends.

Below is a message sent to me from a non-African woman who is married to a Cameroonian man:

> *Greetings, I have become a huge fan of African dishes. I am married to an African and have been introduced to some dishes. My sister-in-law has moved and my husband is not home yet, and I want some of these dishes. Hahahaha. How much are your dishes and how much will it cost to mail the meals to Dothan, AL? I would love to have your cookbook so that I may learn to cook this and surprise my husband when he comes home. Thank you again.*
> *- Shira D. Asolefack, Dothan, AL*

2. I created "Motherland Spices," typically known as "Mammydoro Seasonings," a blend of African herbs and spices and other regular herbs found all over. This makes cooking African food easy because people do not need to wonder where to find the seasonings to acquire the Motherland signature taste. At Motherland, we believe that good, tasty food starts with the right combination of herbs and spices. That is why we have carefully selected the herbs from the African continent and combined them with those in the United States to come up with seasoning blends that give people the right flavors for the foods they make. The seasoning is a click away at www.motherlandspices.com.

3. Most of the younger generation of African descent, born and raised in the West, have not had the luxury of learning these culinary insider tips. They have also missed out on learning from my generation, as their spare time is occupied with other distractions like smartphones, iPads, iPods, and the Internet. Let's not even try to re-enact a three-stone firewood fireplace. They would think, "My parents have lost it and have gone back to caveman days." The world will evolve as it should, so we cannot blame them for lacking this specific skill. This cookbook will help fill that gap for these youngsters.

4. African Americans are now tracing their roots, and there are a good number of them who have visited the country of their ancestors in Africa. Upon their return to the United States, one of the things they miss the most is the cuisine of their forefathers. A lot of them would love to learn how to make the dishes of their ancestors. This cookbook is that part of their heritage.

5. United States Peace Corps volunteers who return home from various countries in Africa tell their stories to family, friends, and other aspiring men and women of this noble cause. Topping the list of their cultural experiences is always the food they ate in their host countries. Having cooked for such events like Meet-up Groups of former Peace Corps and the recruiting events on college campuses, I see the need for a cookbook that is diverse and covers at least one dish per country in Africa. This book will help returning Peace Corps volunteers keep their experiences alive, as they make the foods of their host countries.

Below is a message I received from a Peace Corps volunteer:

> *I just saw your post about recipes. My boyfriend and I have been nominated for the Peace Corps. If we make it all the way in, he would likely be serving in Senegal and I would be in Kenya. We would love to do it up right. Any recipes or suggestions for how to cook our food?*
>
> *- Rosalyn Zock*

6. Everyone is invited to step into the exotic variety of the African cuisine and to taste what we have savored for centuries. We have a culture of cooking our dinners, as opposed to fixing our dinners. I can assure you that a lot of our foods are very healthy. The longer some of the ingredients are cooked, the better they are absorbed into our systems. For example, tomato is a popular thickener used in most of our stews. The longer the tomato is cooked, the better the absorption of lycopene.

7. The ways to cook African food are as diverse as the number of different cultures in Africa. In Africa, we eat almost the same types of foods, but we cook them differently. The recipes in this book are mine. I am not saying they are the best. The only claim I can justifiably make is that they have been tested and have satisfied the taste buds of a cross-section of people, including native Africans, those who have visited the continent, and food adventurers who want to try something new.

APPETIZERS

Appetizers are smaller food portions that come before the main meal. The goal of the appetizer is to stimulate the desire to eat the main meal. In the western world, there are several types of items that fall into this category. In Africa, most appetizers will either be made with pepper or have pepper sauce served as an accompaniment to an appetizer dish. Generally, one would be given "peppersoup" as an appetizer. The soup is both flavorful and spicy, and most Africans believe that the heat awakens the taste buds and the desire to eat. The pepper also helps minimize the effect of alcohol, for those who drink alcohol with their meal.

Gizzards in the Northern region of Cameroon are reserved for the head of the family. In Cameroon, beef is easily affordable to everyone. With the equivalent of a dollar, one can go to the butcher and buy meat that can be used to prepare a meal for four to five people. Conversely, chicken on the other hand costs about three to five dollars and can cost upwards of ten dollars. Chicken is usually reserved for feast days like Christmas, New Year's Day, and other special occasions. Given that there is only one gizzard per chicken, the head of the household gets to enjoy this part of the chicken. As Cameroonians have come abroad, peppered gizzards have become a staple appetizer in all events. The myth behind the gizzards has been dispelled, as anyone can eat as much as they want.

The Portuguese explorers who discovered Cameroon noted the abundance of shrimps in its estuaries and named the land Rio dos Camarões, "River of Shrimp." Shrimps are an integral part of Cameroonian cuisine, but the sad story is that the majority of Cameroonians cannot afford this God-given gift in their meals. It is reserved for the wealthy. So, those who can afford shrimps can serve them as an appetizer in the form of sautéed or grilled shrimps.

Suya, a name for grilled briskets or steaks, is a common appetizer in most parts of West Africa. It is done differently in each country, and the seasoning also varies depending on where it is made. In Cameroon, there are two kinds of suyas—the plain and the peanut-coated suya.

Peppered snails are a delicacy in the Southwestern region of Cameroon and Nigeria. The snails are typically fried or grilled. They are also made in the form of peppersoup. Isiewu (spicy goat head) is an Eastern Nigerian delicacy (Igbo). After cooking the goat head and adding the palm oil and crayfish, a very bitter leaf is sliced and mixed in it. The leaf is called "utazi" in Igbo dialect. Ishiewi is served warm by itself.

ISIEWU

Serves 2

1 goat head
1 cup palm oil
3 habanero fresh peppers
1 small onion
½ cup ground crayfish
2 tablespoon utazi leaves
1 tablespoon uziza leaves
Salt, Maggi, Knorr, or Bouillon cubes to taste
1 teaspoon MammyDoro Achu-Isiewu Seasoning
Akanwu to taste

Cut goat head into pieces, as small as possible. Wash and add salt and Maggi. Dissolve 1 teaspoon of potash in a cup of water and sieve over the pot. Add pepper and onion and cook for about 1½ hours. If possible, start cooking using a pressure cooker for about 45 minutes to reduce prep time. Grind and add crayfish plus 1 teaspoon of MammyDoro Achu-Isiewu Seasoning. Add fresh pepper and continue to cook until well done. When goat head is completely cooked, remove and put in a bowl. Remove the brain and put in a blender. Take skin and flesh off the bones of the goat head and cut into bite sizes. Add a cup of palm oil and a cup of the goat head stock into the blender and stir. Add the pre-cooked peppers and onion into the blender and continue to stir into a thick, creamy, mustard-yellow mixture.

Pour mixture into the bowl containing the goat head pieces and mix properly. If using dry utazi and uziza leaves, soak before beginning the process. Squeeze and add the leaves to the goat head. Slice a bunch of fresh leaves and add to the bowl and mix. Cut onion rings and use for garnishing.

Suggested Serving: Serve as an appetizer.

INGREDIENTS

FINAL DISH

PEPPERED MEAT BALLS

Serves 8

2 lbs. ground beef
1 habanero Pepper
½ cup chopped ginger
½ cup chopped parsley
¼ cup finely chopped onion
¼ cup finely chopped spring onions
¼ cup fresh bread crumbs
1 egg
2 tsp MammyDoro Meat Seasoning
Salt, Bouillon, Knorr or Maggi to taste

Blend the onions, spring onions, ginger, garlic and fresh peppers. Chop parsley and set aside. Beat egg and set aside. In a large bowl, put the ground beef, blended herbs, salt and Maggi, and MammyDoro Meat Seasoning. Add bread crumbs, and egg and mix. Add chopped parsley and green peppers and mix. Form the mixture into desired-sized meatballs and place on a tray. Put water in a cooking pot and add 1 teaspoon of salt. Bring water to the boil and place meatballs in boiling water. Cook for about 10 minutes. In a frying pan, add ½ cup vegetable oil and heat. Pour ¼ cup chopped onions in oil. Remove and place meatballs in oil. This is not deep-frying. This is just to make them brown since the meatballs are already pre-cooked. The pre-cooking reduces the grease from the meat.

Serving Suggestion: When meatballs are done, place in a plate and serve
Add pepper sauce to the side if more pepper is needed.

INGREDIENTS

FINAL DISH

A BOOK OF RECIPES, NUTRITIONAL INFORMATION & EDUCATION

SAUTEED OR BBQ SHRIMPS

½ cup vegetable oil, preferably olive oil
1 teaspoon MammyDoro Fish & Shrimp Seasoning
1 teaspoon MammyDoro Vegetable Seasoning
1 large onion
½ cup chopped parsley
1 tablespoon olive
Raw shrimps, as needed
Salt, Maggi, Bouillon, or Knorr cubes to taste

Sautéed Shrimps

Peel and wash shrimps with lemon or lime juice and rinse properly. Add salt, Maggi, and MammyDoro Seafood Seasoning. Let it sit for at least 20 minutes. Chop up onions and parsley. In a saucepan, add ½ cup of vegetable oil and heat for 2 minutes. Add onions and stir for about 5 minutes. Add seasoned shrimps, stir, and add chopped parsley. When shrimps turn pink, remove and serve.

BBQ Shrimps

Soak bamboo skewers in water for about an hour to prevent burning. Cut up onion and bell peppers in 1 inch cubes. Put in a mixing bowl and add a pinch of salt, Maggi, Bouillon, or Knorr cubes to taste. Add one tablespoon of olive oil and mix. Season the shrimps as described above. Place shrimps on skewer and alternate each shrimp with a cube of onion and bell peppers. Place on the grill on very low heat. Shrimps cook fast and can lose their moisture if cooked on high heat. They become very tough. Use a brush to rub the oil and seasonings at the bottom of the bowl while cooking the shrimps. When pink, turn and cook the other side. Serve warm.

Serving Suggestion: Serve with hot sauce or any sauce of choice.

INGREDIENTS

FINAL DISH

STIR FRIED PEPPERED GIZZARDS

Serves 6

3 lbs. gizzards
½ cup vegetable oil
1 teaspoon MammyDoro Meat Seasoning
1 cup mixed chopped ginger, onions and leeks
½ teaspoon freshly ground black pepper
Salt to taste
Maggi, Bouillon, or Knorr cubes to taste
Pepper to taste

Wash the gizzards, put them in a pot, and add water and salt. Cook for about 20 minutes and strain—gizzards are usually gammy. Put gizzards back into pot. Blend ginger, garlic, onions, pepper, and add to gizzards. Adjust seasonings to taste and mix properly. Add MammyDoro Meat Seasoning, 1 cup of vegetable oil, and water enough to cook gizzards. Cook until gizzards are tender and water dries up

Serving Suggestion: Use a cooking spoon and place on a small plate. Add pepper sauce to the side if more pepper is needed.

INGREDIENTS

FINAL DISH

SUYA OR SOYA

Serves 6

2 lbs Goat meat
1 lb chicken breast
2 lbs beef
1 large Onion
3 bell peppers

Maggi, Bouillon or Knorr cubes to taste
MammyDoro Meat Seasoning
MammyDoro Chicken Seasoning
MammyDoro Vegetable Seasoning
Vegetable oil

If using charcoal, which is the preferred and best method to make suya, light the grill and let the wood burn for about 30 minutes to reduce the amount of toxins from the lighter fluid and charcoal. What is needed is the heat to cook the meat and not the flame. The process of making suya is similar to the American BBQ method.

Goat Suya or Lamb Suya

Cube the onions and bell peppers and put into a bowl. Add a pinch of salt and 1 teaspoon MammyDoro Vegetable Seasoning and set aside. Cut meat into bite sizes. Place in a pot, add a teaspoon of salt, and bring to a boil for 20 minutes Strain and put into a bowl. Add 1 teaspoon of salt, 1 teaspoon of MammyDoro Meat Seasoning, 1 Maggi or Knorr cube, or ½ Bouillon cube and ¼ cup vegetable oil. Mix properly and place the meat on a grilling pan. Put on the grill or put the pieces on skewers, placing the sliced vegetables between each piece of meat. Grill until well done.

Beef

Slice beef in ½-inch thick pieces. Place in a bowl. Add 1 teaspoon of salt, 1 teaspoon of MammyDoro Meat Seasoning, 1 Maggi or Knorr cube or ½ Bouillon cube, and ¼ cup vegetable oil. Mix properly. Let marinate for an hour. Place the meat on the grill or put the pieces on skewers if need be. Generally, the peanut-coated suya meat is placed on skewers and the meat is cut into very thin pieces before marinating. Add MammyDoro Meat Seasoning as well as MammyDoro Peanut Mix. Cook until meat is well done.

Chicken Suya

This is made in a similar way to the beef suya. You want to marinate for a longer period because chicken breasts that are commonly used for chicken suya do not have any marrow, which gives extra flavor to the meat. Slice and marinate the chicken with MammyDoro Chicken Seasoning. Continue the process like you would beef suya.

Suggested Serving: Serve with chopped onions, tomatoes and hot sauce or Kankan Soya pepper.

INGREDIENTS

FINAL DISH

BEANS

Beans contain mostly soluble fiber, which can help decrease blood cholesterol levels and therefore may help reduce the risk of heart disease. Soluble fiber may also help patients with diabetes maintain improved blood sugar levels because the fiber helps to slow the rate of absorption of carbohydrates. Most beans, including black-eyed peas, are a rich source of iron. Iron is an essential component of one of the proteins found in the red blood cells, which carry oxygen to all body tissues. Navy beans and other beans, such as pinto beans and black beans, are all known scientifically as Phaseolus vulgaris. They are also referred to as "common beans" probably because they all derived from a common bean ancestor that originated in Peru. An inexpensive form of good protein, they have become popular in many cultures throughout the world. According to Whfoods.com, the largest commercial producers of dried common beans, including the navy bean, are India, China, Indonesia, Brazil, and the United States. Beans can be used as a protein source instead of an animal food. In fact, many vegetarians use legumes to substitute for meat when planning meals. One serving of black-eyed peas is equal to one-half cup. One serving of black-eyed peas contains 70 calories, making it a low-calorie option when served without additional condiments. And, these beans do not contain any fat or cholesterol.

Black-eyed peas are especially rich in potassium. This mineral is important for the proper function of all cells, tissues, and organs in the body. It is also crucial for heart function and plays a key role in muscle contraction. Zinc is another mineral found in black-eyed peas. Zinc is involved in many aspects of cellular metabolism and is therefore essential for the immune function, protein synthesis, wound healing, and healthy cell division. Black-eyed peas are white legumes with a small black dot, and this characteristic appearance, resembling an eye, is how they get their name. These delicious beans are well known in Southern and Southwestern cooking in the United States. The nutrition of the black-eyed pea makes it an excellent addition to any menu. Hoppin John is a delicacy of the South, especially Savanah, Georgia. It is a dish of black-eyed peas and rice, eaten every New Years, and the meat is an integral part of this dish. These meats include hog jowl, ham hocks, neckbone, cracklings—smoked, fatty meats. Not trying to be offensive to true Savannahians, I am going to present a vegetarian version of Hoppin John. I am sure there are lots of vegetarians who feel left out from this Southern tradition. This is your time to enjoy Hoppin John without missing the meat. It is believed that Hoppin John originated from Senegambia (Senegal/Gambia). The slaves who arrived in the South from these countries brought this cuisine with them. In Senegal and Gambia, black-eyed peas and rice are cooked with smoked fish. This dish is called Tchebu-ketiahk.

Black-eyed peas are a very popular type of bean in Nigeria. It is actually a delicacy, and it is not uncommon to find the average Nigerian unaccustomed to any other type of beans beyond black-eyed peas. In Nigeria, it is used in making Moi Moi, Acara, and made in a stew form as well. Lentils and split peas are popular in Ethiopian cuisine. These are cooked in a stew to accompany the main dish—injera. Cameroon is Africa in miniature. If you find it anywhere in African, it will be found in Cameroon. This is also true about all species of beans. The North West Region of Cameroon grows all species of beans that can be found on the continent. Beans in general are also popular in Cameroon. It is very common to find a group of people standing at road sides early in the morning before work or school starts buying a typical breakfast of beans and puff puff (beignets-aricots). In the evenings, the sellers who take a break between breakfast and dinner are seen serving the same dishes at road sides. The recipe for this commercial version is very basic and easy. In boarding schools all around the country, beans are a main source of protein for the students, even though most of them hate the days of the week when beans are served because they complain that weevils are found in the beans. It is not uncommon to attend a Cameroonian party in the diaspora and Beans and Puff Puff are the most sought out amongst Cameroonians. It has become a delicacy.

Jahica rice is my version of the Caribbean Red Peas & Rice. I have given this dish a Cameroonian touch with MammyDoro Beans seasoning. Using a combination of the Jamaican and Haitian methods, I have come up with a dish that incorporates all three cultures. In Jamaica, coconut milk is part of the ingredients, whilst in Haiti cloves are a must have in the riz colle. Therefore, I combined the Cameroonian coconut rice recipe, coconut milk, cloves, and the MammyDoro Beans Seasoning to make Jahica rice. Corn chaff is also a common dish in Cameroon. It is to Cameroon as Red Peas & Rice is to the Caribbean. So like the name implies, it is a dish of beans and corn. This is a pescetarian dish, as it is cooked with smoked fish and crayfish. It is absolutely delicious, and the flavor is outstanding due to the addition of the bush onion or country onion. The combination of beans and corn (makande) is also popular in many parts of Tanzania. Lentils, like other beans, are rich in dietary fiber, both the soluble and insoluble type. Soluble fiber forms a gel-like substance in the digestive tract that snares bile (which contains cholesterol) and ferries it out of the body. Insoluble fiber not only helps to increase stool bulk and prevent constipation but also helps prevent digestive disorders, such as irritable bowel syndrome and diverticulosis. To boil lentils, use three cups of liquid for each cup of lentils. Lentils placed in already boiling water will be easier to digest than those that were brought to a boil with the water. When the water returns to a boil, turn down the heat to simmer and cover. Ethiopians eat a variety of lentils with injera.

CORN CHAFF

(Red beans and corn) - Serves 10

4 cups beans
1 cup chopped onion
1 red bell pepper
¼ cup garlic
1 cup ground crayfish (optional)
2 teaspoons MammyDoro Beans Seasoning
2 cups mixed chopped parsley, cilantro, and basil
Salt, Maggi, Bouillon, or Knorr cubes to taste
4 cups corn
1 cup chopped leeks
½ cup ginger
10 roma tomatoes
2 cups vegetable oil

Open the cans of corn and beans, strain and rinse properly, and set aside. Blend basil, parsley, cilantro, leeks, red bell pepper, ginger, and garlic and set aside. Chop tomatoes and onions and set aside.

Put oil into a saucepan and heat for about 3 minutes on medium-high heat. Add ground crayfish (if used) to heated oil and stir. Add chopped onions and continue to stir for about 5 minutes, then add chopped tomatoes and continue to stir for another 10 minutes. Pour blended herbs into pot and stir. Add 2 Maggi or Knorr cubes or 1 Bouillon cube and 1 teaspoon of salt. Mix properly and add 4 cups water. Let cook for about 45 minutes, stirring constantly and adding water ½ cup at a time to prevent sticking. Add corn and beans, 2 teaspoons MammyDoro Beans Seasoning, and 1 teaspoon of curry. Reduce heat to low and keep stirring for another 10 minutes until water dries up to desired consistency. Taste and adjust seasonings. Optionally fry onions using ½ cup of oil and pour into pot to enhance flavor.

Note: If dry corn and beans are used, pre-cook them before adding to sauce.

Suggested Serving: Serve warm.

INGREDIENTS

FINAL DISH

LENTILS & LIVER

Serves 12

4 cups dried green, brown, or French lentils
1 lb. beef liver
2 cups chopped onions
½ cup chopped leeks or green onions
1 cup mix chopped parsley, basil, and cilantro
4 roma tomatoes
1 teaspoon MammyDoro Beans Seasoning
1 teaspoon salt
2 cups vegetable oil
½ teaspoon curry
Salt, Maggi, Bouillon or Knorr cubes to taste
Pepper to taste

Cut liver into bite sizes, rinse and set aside. Blend ginger, garlic, parsley, basil, cilantro, leeks and tomatoes and set aside. Pick and remove any shriveled lentils, debris, or rocks from the lentils. Thoroughly wash lentils under running water. Bring 8 cups of water to the boil and pour in lentils. Add 1 teaspoon of salt and ½ teaspoon of baking soda. Cook over high heat for 10 minutes; reduce the heat to a very gentle simmer for 3 minutes. Remove pot from the stove, strain and set aside.

In another pot, add 2 cups of cooking oil and heat for 2 minutes. Add chopped onions and liver, 1 teaspoon of salt, 2 Maggi or Knorr or 1 Bouillon cube. Add 1 teaspoon MammyDoro Meat Seasoning and stir for 15 minutes. Add blended herbs and cook for 20 minutes and add precooked lentils and mix properly. Add 1 teaspoon MammyDoro Beans Seasoning and ½ teaspoon of curry. Optionally, fry 1 cup chopped onions in ½ cup of oil and add to lentils to enhance flavor. Let simmer for 5 minutes and serve.

Suggested Serving: Serve with Injera, steam rice or other starch.

INGREDIENTS

Lentils
Lentejas

FINAL DISH

A BOOK OF RECIPES, NUTRITIONAL INFORMATION & EDUCATION

STEWED BEANS

(Black-eyed peas)

5 cups dry beans
1 red bell pepper
½ cup ginger
¼ cup garlic
10 roma (plum) tomatoes
2 cups vegetable oil
½ cup ground crayfish (optional)
2 cups mixed chopped parsley, cilantro, basil
1 cup chopped onion and 1 cup chopped leeks
2 teaspoons MammyDoro Beans Seasoning
Salt, Maggi, Bouillon, or Knorr cubes to taste

Soak dried beans for 2 hours. This makes for faster cooking. Blend basil, parsley, cilantro, leeks, bell pepper, ginger, and garlic and set aside. Chop tomatoes and onions and set aside. Rinse beans and put in a large pot. Add 5 cups water, 1 teaspoon of salt, 2 teaspoons MammyDoro Beans Seasoning, 2 Maggi or Knorr cubes or 1 Bouillon cube, and cook for 35 minutes.
Pour oil in another saucepan and heat for about 2 minutes on high-medium heat. Add ground crayfish (if used) to heated oil and stir. Add chopped onions and continue to stir for about 5 minutes, then add chopped tomatoes and continue to stir for another 5 minutes. Pour blended herbs into pot and stir. Add 2 Maggi/Knorr cubes or 1 Bouillon cube and 1 teaspoon of salt. Let cook for about 45 minutes, stirring constantly and adding water ½ a cup at a time to prevent sticking. Strain the pre-cooked beans from stock and add into sauce. Add 1 teaspoon of curry. Reduce heat to low and keep stirring for another 5 minutes until water dries up to desired consistency.

Note: If canned beans are used, rinse properly before adding to sauce to remove excess salt and preservatives. Taste and adjust seasonings.

Suggested Serving: Serve with steamed rice, potatoes or fried plantains.

INGREDIENTS

FINAL DISH

STEWED BEANS

(Red Beans) - Serves 8

4 cups dry beans
1 cup chopped leeks
1 habanero pepper (optional)
¼ cup garlic
½ cup ground crayfish (optional)
2 teaspoons MammyDoro Beans Seasoning
2 cups mixed chopped parsley, cilantro, and basil
Salt, Maggi, Bouillon, or Knorr cubes to taste
1 cup chopped onion
1 red bell pepper
½ cup ginger
10 roma (plum) tomatoes
2 cups vegetable oil
½ teaspoon baking soda

Bring water to a boil in a large pot and add dry beans. Do not soak in advance. Add 2 teaspoons of salt and ½ teaspoon of akanwa (potash) or baking soda. Let the beans cook for 30 minutes. Strain, rinse, and set aside.

Blend basil, parsley, cilantro, leeks, bell pepper, ginger, garlic, onion, red bell pepper, and tomatoes and set aside. Put beans into a saucepan and add 7 cups water, 1 teaspoon of salt, 2 teaspoons MammyDoro Beans Seasoning, 2 Maggi/Knorr cubes or 1 Bouillon cube, and cook for 30 minutes. Add the blended herbs. Add 2 cups palm oil into a frying pan and heat for 2 minutes. Add crayfish and stir. Add blended herbs. Cook for 10 minutes and pour sauce into the beans. Add 1 teaspoon of curry and continue to cook for another 45 minutes. Taste and adjust seasonings as needed.

Note: If canned beans are used, rinse properly before adding to sauce to remove excess salt and preservatives. Taste and adjust seasonings.

Suggested Serving: Serve with steamed rice, potatoes or fried plantains.

INGREDIENTS

FINAL DISH

SALT

The American Diabetes Association recommends that people with diabetes complications should aim at 2300 mg of salt or less per day. One teaspoon of table salt is 2,350 mg. So the total amount of salt recommended in all meals per day should be a little less than a teaspoon. If you already have high blood pressure, that number should be even less. When you use salt-free seasonings like Motherland Spices in cooking your favorite foods, you can control the amount of salt you add to your food. What truly adds flavor to your food is the natural aroma from herbs and spices properly combined to serve each food type. It is not the salt, or worse still, the monosodium glutamate (MSG). Some studies have concluded that MSG is the silent killer in your kitchen's cabinet. I, personally, have been a victim, with unexplained headaches and dizziness that could not be cured with medications. These only stopped when I read the labels on each spice I had in my kitchen cabinet and unfortunately had to discard all of them due to the presence of MSG in the blends. MSG has been described as the worst food additive on the market. It activates the taste buds and makes them more receptive to flavor, whereas it is bad for your brain. In Cameroon and Nigeria it is called "aginomoto," or Chinese salt. Too much salt, or MSG, is detrimental to your health, especially if you are already suffering from other diseases. High salt intake will raise your blood pressure and may lead to heart attack. There are some salt substitutes available that you may use, but some may contain a high amount of potassium, so you may want to check with your physician to make sure the excess potassium does not complicate things even further. Most excess salt is found in packaged foods, so the best way to reduce and control your salt intake is to cook your own food and also used salt-free herbs, which automatically increase the flavor of your foods and do not require the addition of excess salt.

FONIO

Fonio is considered the oldest grain in Africa and among the world's fastest maturing cereals. It produces grains from 6 to 8 weeks after being planted, and it is ready to be harvested long before most other grains. It is the staple food of the people of Guinea and Mali and also widely consumed in Senegal and Sierra Leone. It is grown in all West African countries, from Senegal to Nigeria, with the exception of Liberia. It is evident that this crop can withstand the arid lands of the Sub-Saharan region since it grows in the more arid lands of the fonio-growing nations. Fonio is widely cultivated across the Fouta Djallon Plateau of Guinea because it can grow on acidic soil that is harmful to other crops. The farmers in Sierra Leone turn to the cultivation of fonio when there is insufficient rainfall to facilitate the growth of much needed rice. It is a great substitute for this rice-loving people. Most of the rain is in the southern parts of the country.

Fonio's consistency is a cross between quinoa and couscous, and it is also gluten free. It is very nutritious and contains amino acids. It can be cooked as couscous and served with peanut butter stew or mixed with vegetables as a salad. It may become the new super grain, competing with quinoa. Although the nutritive value of fonio is high, this grain has not been given the exposure it deserves, and farming of it is not yet at industrial levels.

DOUGHS & FRITTERS

For many kids, there is no worse breakfast than oatmeal. They will eat pancakes, waffles, and cereal, but they won't touch oatmeal. Many kids and adults do not realize that one bowl of oatmeal a day can keep the doctor away. It is full of fiber, and just one cup contains almost 26 micrograms of folate, with more than 10 grams of protein.

Oatmeal contains a certain type of fiber called beta-gluten fiber. This fiber protects against heart disease and also revs up the immune system. It helps the immune cells seek out and repair areas of the body that may be fighting a bacterial infection. Since oatmeal is high in fiber and consequently good for your heart, it offers many cardiovascular benefits, which includes a reduced risk of developing high blood pressure. It is recommended that postmenopausal women with high blood pressure eat six servings of oatmeal or other whole grains on a weekly basis. Studies show that men can also reduce their risk of heart failure if they eat one bowl of whole grain cereal or oatmeal a day.

It is good to change the method of eating this wonder grain to eliminate the monotony. Your child will also love this with a glass of milk or juice before heading off to school. He or she will be loaded with the energy needed for the day.

Quinoa, pronounced "keen-wah," is not related to wheat or grain. It is gluten free. Millions of people are discovering that they feel better and lose weight when they introduce gluten free grains or products to their diet. Quinoa is a complex carbohydrate, with a low glycemic index. It is also a good source of riboflavin, which helps reduce the frequency of attacks in migraine sufferers. This occurs by improving the energy metabolism within the brain and muscle cells. There is a belief that this super grain helps the production of breast milk, since quinoa is a good source of lysine, an essential amino acid for creating protein. It is also a good source of phosphorus, zinc, copper, manganese, B6, niacin, thiamin, and dietary fiber. A hungry baby is a fussy baby and hard to soothe, so if you plan to breastfeed your new-born, then quinoa should be top on your shopping list.

Quinoa has a bitter taste and a slightly pungent smell. Quinoa is ideal for those suffering from allergies to the grass family, since it is a leafy plant seed. There are several ways of preparing the seeds. I have come up with a pancake recipe with quinoa flour that completely takes away the smell and bitter taste, and leaves you with the crunchy taste of the oatmeal and quinoa mix. It is very filling and provides the nutrients to start your day. The quinoa pilaf is another great alternative to rice pilaf.

Injera is a large sourdough flatbread that is typically about 50 centimeters (20") in diameter and is made out of fermented teff flour. It has a slightly spongy texture. Due to the fermentation process in making injera, the final product tastes sour. It is the national dish of Ethiopia and Eritrea. A similar variant of this dough is eaten in Somalia and Djibouti called (conjeero or lehooh) and Sudan. The grain from which injera is made is one of the recommended grains that are gluten-free. It is a healthy alternative to bread flour.

Injera is eaten with a variety of stews (meat or fish), soups, and salad. Small pieces of the dough are torn and used to grab the stew or salad, or soaked into the soup before eating. Ethiopian cuisine generally consists of vegetables and spicy meat dishes, which usually come in the form of wat (stew). The injera under the stew soaks up the juices and flavors. In the United States, injera can be bought in grocery stores and restaurants specializing in Eritrean, Ethiopian, and Somali foods. All you will have to make is the different stews that are eaten with injera.

Garbanzo beans are fantastic for providing our digestive system with nutrients. No food macronutrients are more valuable for blood sugar regulation than fiber and protein. Garbanzos are rich in these nutrients and, therefore, a food you definitely want to keep on your "digestive support" list—especially if you are focusing on the colon. Between 65-75% of the fiber found in garbanzo beans is insoluble fiber, which remains undigested. Beans are also gluten free and a good choice for those wanting to live a happy, healthy, gluten-free life.

CASSAVA FRITTERS

(Akara Banana) - Serves 6   #themotherlandcookbook

5 - 6 over-ripe bananas
2 lbs. grated cassava
1 cup of gari (or enough to bind)
½ - 1 flat teaspoon of sea salt or kosher salt
1 tablespoon sugar
½ - 1 flat teaspoon of nutmeg, cinnamon, or vanilla (optional)
Vegetable frying oil

Peel and mash over-ripe bananas in a bowl. Use a potato masher. You can also use a food processor but let mixture be like orange juice with pulp, not like a smoothie if you use a food processor. Add grated cassava into the bowl and mix properly. Add salt and nutmeg into the mixture. Add gari a bit at a time and mix and continue adding until desired texture—not hard. Leave for at least 20 minutes for gari to soak and rise. Mold into desired shapes (either round or oblong) and place on a tray. Heat up oil to about 400 degrees and start deep frying. Each batch takes about 4 minutes depending on how hot the oil is. Oil should be very hot to prevent fritters from soaking oil and coming out mushy.

Note: The banana quantity should be relative to the dryness of the gari that you use in binding. Some gari is dryer than others and may require more bananas. If the gari you use is not too dry, then 5 bananas should be enough.

Suggested Serving: Serve hot with hot sauce.

INGREDIENTS

Dayella Lima

FINAL DISH

BLACK-EYED PEAS FRITTERS

(Akara Beans)

2 cups dried black-eyed peas
1 onion
½ cup chopped chives
½ teaspoon salt
1 habanero, finely chopped (optional)
Vegetable oil for frying

Put the black-eyed peas a cup or two at a time into a blender. Add 3 cups water and whip enough to break the peas in half and pour into a large bowl. Continue the process until all the peas are cracked. Let it sit overnight for the peas to soak up water and become soft and fresh again. The next day, rub peas together between your palms to remove the skins. Rinse to wash away the skin and black eyes and drain in a colander.

Chop up onions, pepper, and chives and add to the washed black-eyed peas. Use a food processor to grind them to a thick paste. Add only ¼ cup of water because the more water you add, the more the paste breaks when dipped into hot oil during frying. Add salt and pepper (optional) and mix properly. Use a hand mixer to mix and aerate until mixture is smooth and fluffy.

Put frying oil into a deep frying pan or wok and heat for 5 - 10 minutes. Depending on the size of the fritters, use a teaspoon, tablespoon, or ice cream scoop to measure the batter and drop into the hot oil. Drop 1 tablespoon of mixture into the hot oil and fry for about 5 minutes, or until golden brown. Re-adjust the heat level if necessary and continue frying. Fry the fritters until they are golden brown. Turn when the side in the oil becomes golden brown. Remove the akara from the oil with a slotted spoon and drain on a paper towel. Serve immediately.

Suggested Serving: Serve hot as a pass item at cocktails; as a snack or with bread, puff puff or akamu for breakfast.

CORN MEAL FRITTERS

(Beignets mais) - Serves 3

1 over ripe bananas
½ cup corn meal
¼ cup flour
1 teaspoon brown sugar
   cup of water
Vegetable oil for frying
Pinch of salt
½ teaspoon yeast
Pinch of nutmeg or cinnamon (optional)

Dissolve yeast, salt, and sugar in water and set aside. Peel bananas, slice into a bowl, and mash with a wooden spoon. Add nutmeg or cinnamon and mix properly. Add corn meal and mix. Add flour, mix, and pour in dissolved yeast, salt, and sugar. Mix properly (using a mixer) and cover the container with plastic wrap to keep the heat in and let the yeast rise. To have a good texture, keep for 2 hours.

Heat oil for about 15 minutes on high heat and then reduce to medium heat and start frying the fritters. Take off plastic, mix the dough, and use a tablespoon or teaspoon to scoop the dough and drop into the hot oil. Cook each batch for about 5 minutes or until dark brown and cooked through. Drain on kitchen paper towel.

Suggested Serving: Serve preferably hot with hot pepper sauce.

INGREDIENTS

FINAL DISH

DOUGHNUTS

1½ cups milk
2 eggs
4 cups all-purpose flour (not self-rise)
½ cup sugar
2 teaspoons baking powder
½ teaspoon salt
½ teaspoon nutmeg
1 stick unsalted butter
Vegetable oil, for frying

Instruments
Small ice cream scoop
Electric hand mixer

Cream the butter and sugar until fluffy. Add flour, salt, baking powder, and nutmeg and stir. In a small bowl, whisk together the milk and the egg and add to mixture. Stir or use hand mixer to whisk until mixture is smooth. Let the mixture sit for at least 20 minutes before frying. Line a baking sheet or large bowl with paper towels. Add vegetable oil to a large pot and heat to 350° F. Once the oil has reached 350° F, use a small ice cream scoop to drop about 1 tablespoon scoops of dough into the oil, careful not to overcrowd the pot. If you use a larger ice scream scoop, measure just half. The size of the ice scream scoop determines the size of the doughnut. Leave room for doughnut to flip and form while frying.   Fry the doughnut, flipping them in the oil for about 2 minutes or until each side is golden brown. You will know that the level of heat is adequate when the doughnuts flip without you touching them. Using a slotted spoon, transfer the doughnut to the paper towel-lined bowl or baking sheet and let cool.

Suggested Serving: Serve as pass item at a cocktail party.

INGREDIENTS

FINAL DISH

FALAFEL

(Gluten-free Egyptian Akara)

4 cups garbanzo beans
1 cup chopped Italian parsley
1 cup chopped onion
¼ teaspoon cayenne pepper
½ cup of garbanzo flour
1 teaspoon salt or to taste
½ teaspoon freshly ground black pepper
Grape seed oil for frying

2 cups of fava beans
2 cups chopped cilantro
½ cup of chopped garlic
1 teaspoon coriander
1 teaspoon cumin
½ cup water
1 teaspoon baking powder
1 cup green onions

If you cannot find peeled fava beans, use the non-peeled and soak the garbanzo and fava beans overnight. The fava beans are easy to peel when properly soaked. Peel the eye first and squeeze the bean out of the shell. Strain, rinse, and blend the garbanzo beans using a food processor until crumbly, not pureed. They should not grind to a puree like the fava beans. Pour mixture into a bowl. Blend the fava beans with ½ cup of water together with the onions, green onions, cilantro, and garlic and combine with the ground garbanzo beans. Add garbanzo bean flour and mix properly. Add all the other seasonings and mix properly. Taste and adjust seasonings.

Put oil in a frying pan or wok and set on medium to high heat. Use a falafel maker to mold the falafels or two tablespoons, one to scoop and the other to shape the falafel. Shape and drop into the hot oil. Cook until golden brown, then flip to cook the other side. Using a slotted spoon, remove the falafel and place on a paper towel to soak up extra oil.

Suggested Serving: Serve with pita bread, tahini, or any hot sauce and salad; serve warm; do not let cool because it loses its crispiness (If heated, after a while it becomes rubbery.)

INGREDIENTS

FINAL DISH

GARBANZO-FAVA BEANS FRITTERS

(Garbanzo-fava beans flour) - Serves 6

2 cups garbanzo-fava beans flour
1¼ cup water
Pinch of salt and pinch of Knorr powder
¼ cup finely chopped spring onions or chives
¼ cup chopped onions
1 teaspoon baking powder
1 teaspoon freshly ground black pepper or to taste
Habanero pepper to taste (optional)

Measure bean flour and put in mixing bowl. Add salt, freshly ground black pepper, Knorr powder, and baking powder. Add water and mix properly using a wooden spoon. Add chopped spring onions or chives and ground habanero pepper (if desired). Use a hand mixer to whip mixture properly for about 3 minutes. Cover and let the mixture sit for 30 minutes. Pour frying oil into a deep frying pot and heat for 5 minutes. Scoop and fry garbanzo-fava bean fritters using a tablespoon or teaspoon. The size will depend on the spoon used to scoop the mixture for frying. When one side is golden brown, flip to cook the other side. Remove and place on paper towel.

Suggested Serving: Serve hot, with pap, akamu, hot sauce or as a pass item at any cocktail party.

OATMEAL-QUINOA FRITTERS

(Banana) - Serves 6   #themotherlandcookbook

1 overripe banana
1 cup oatmeal flour or brown rice flour
1 cup quinoa flour
1 cup milk
2 teaspoons sugar
1/2 teaspoon nutmeg
1/2 teaspoon baking powder
1 egg
1 pinch of Sea salt
Frying oil

Peel bananas and place into a large bowl. Mash them until smooth. Add sugar, milk, salt, nutmeg, baking powder and mix properly. Add flour and mix until the "batter" just barely runs off of the spoon. If it is too thick, it will be too heavy when fried. Heat oil in a deep frying pan for about 5 minutes. Use ice scream scoop and scoop just half full and drop in hot oil. You know the level of heat is right when the fritter flip over automatically when one side is brown. When the edges are brown, turn over and cook the opposite side. The fritters will be dark brown in color due to the bananas, but yummy and healthy. Drain onto paper towels.

Suggested Serving: Serve warm with coffee, tea, juice or just water.

INGREDIENTS

FINAL DISH

A BOOK OF RECIPES, NUTRITIONAL INFORMATION & EDUCATION

OATMEAL-QUINOA PANCAKES

Serves 4

1 cup of oatmeal flour or brown rice flour
1 cup of quinoa flour
1 ripe banana
pinch of salt
pinch of baking powder or 1 egg (white only)
1½ cup of milk
½ teaspoon of nutmeg

Peel and put banana in a blender. Add salt, nutmeg, baking powder or egg white, and sugar. Blend into a fine puree. Measure flour and put in a mixing bowl and pour in mixture. Mix thoroughly giving a running mixture. Let sit for at least 5 minutes. Scoop in ½ cup at a time and fry in a flat frying pan using a teaspoon of frying oil for each pancake or another frying oil of choice. The wider the frying pan the lighter the pancakes.

Suggested Serving: Serve with coffee, tea, juice or just plain water.

INGREDIENTS

Melanie Musa

FINAL DISH

A BOOK OF RECIPES, NUTRITIONAL INFORMATION & EDUCATION

PUFF PUFF

(Beignets - Regular flour)

2 lbs. all-purpose flour (preferably Gold Medal)
2 teaspoons or 2 sachets of active dry yeast
1 flat teaspoon of salt
¾ cup sugar
3¼ cups lukewarm water
Vegetable oil for frying

Pour lukewarm water into a deep container. Add salt, sugar, and yeast. Stir until all dissolves. Add flour gradually and mix briskly until smooth. Keep mixing using hand or wooden spoon until mixture bounces when you scoop and drop back into container. Cover mixture with plastic-wrap tightly to keep the heat inside the container. When the top of the mixture is full of bubbles (for better consistency keep for about 2 hours) it is ready for frying.

Pour frying oil into a wok, deep fryer or pot and heat on medium to high for about 15 minutes. Drop a little bit in hot oil and wait for it to fry and rise to top (this is the check-heat level test). Remove from oil and start frying the rest of the puff puff if the test puff puff flips around by itself To fry, close fingers and remove mixture by rolling up on the skin of the container, squeeze, and drop into oil. When they start getting brown, use a fork and shake them for all to turn; if heat is at the right level you know because the balls will flip by themselves. If you are unable to cut the dough and fry, try using an ice scream scoop. The size of the puff puff will depend on the size of the ice scream scoop.

Suggested Serving: Serve warm or hot with coffee, tea or stewed beans or with hot sauce.

INGREDIENTS

FINAL DISH

PUFF PUFF

(Beignets - Gluten free flour)

1 lb. gluten free flour
1 teaspoon or 1 sachet of active dry yeast
½ teaspoon of salt
½ cup sugar
2½ cups lukewarm water
1 teaspoon xantham gum
Vegetable oil for frying

Pour lukewarm water into a deep container. Add salt, sugar, and yeast. Stir until all dissolves. Add flour gradually and mix briskly until smooth. Add egg and gum and continue to mix. Keep mixing using hand or wooden spoon until mixture is smooth. It will not really bounce much because gluten free flour does not hold that much moisture. Cover mixture with plastic-wrap tightly to keep the heat inside the container. Keep for about 2½ hours. Pour frying oil into a wok or fryer and heat for about 15 minutes. Drop a little bit in hot oil and wait for it to fry and rise to top (this is the check-heat level test). Remove from oil and start frying the rest if the test puff puff flips around by itself . To fry, close fingers and remove mixture by rolling up on the inner wall of the container, squeeze, and drop into oil. When puff puff starts getting brown, use a fork and shake them for all to flip; if heat is at the right level you will know because the balls flip by themselves. If you are unable to cut the dough and fry, try using an ice scream scoop.

Suggested Serving: Serve warm or hot with coffee, tea or stewed beans or with hot sauce.

INGREDIENTS

FINAL DISH

PATTI DOUGH

(Regular Flour)

6 cups unsalted flour
2 teaspoons of sea salt
1 teaspoon baking powder
1½ cups water
1¼ sticks unsalted butter
2 eggs

Put flour into a mixing bowl. Add butter, salt, and egg yolk to flour. Rub in until flour and butter are completely mixed. Make a hole in the middle of the flour and pour in water. Start mixing small portions until flour is completely mixed. Cut chunks of dough and bread mixture on a flat surface until smooth. Wrap dough in a kitchen towel and keep in a refrigerator for an hour. Remove dough from refrigerator, cut chunks, and flatten. Cut into desired sizes and fill in with pre-cooked beef, fish, chicken, turkey, or veggie filling.

Note: If dough is kept in a freezer for future use, when needed, defrost naturally before kneading and rolling. The number depends on size of patties.

INGREDIENTS

FINAL DISH

PATTI DOUGH

(Gluten Free Flour)

4 cups gluten-free
2 teaspoons of salt
1 cup ice cold water
6 flat teaspoons xanthan gum
1½ stick unsalted butter
1 teaspoon of baking powder
2 eggs

Put flour into a mixing bowl. Add butter, salt, egg yolks, and gum to flour. Rub in until flour and butter are completely mixed. Make a hole in the middle of the flour and pour in water. Start mixing small portions until flour is completely mixed. Cut chunks of dough and bread mixture on a flat surface until smooth. Wrap dough in a kitchen towel and keep in a refrigerator for an hour. Remove dough from refrigerator, cut into four parts, and thread properly until smooth. Cut into desired sizes and fill as needed.

Note: If dough is kept in a freezer for future use, when needed, defrost naturally before kneading and rolling. The number really depends on size of patties.

INGREDIENTS

FINAL DISH

GLUTEN

Nowadays there is a lot of chatter about gluten and gluten free foods. The FDA defines gluten as a mixture of proteins that occur naturally in wheat, rye, barley, and cross-breeds of these grains. It can cause significant harm to many people. Dr. Davis and Dr. Brownstein believe a gluten-free or reduced gluten diet would benefit most people, especially those suffering from digestive problems, thyroid problems, autoimmune disorders, arthritis, diabetes, and even fatigue. In his book, Wheat Belly, cardiologist Dr. William Davis explains, "it's not excess fat intake or too little exercise that is making us fat." He says the culprit is today's genetically engineered wheat—and the agri-business that pushes it on us in every aisle of the grocery store—and your only defense is a gluten-free diet. Gluten free foods are made with grains other than wheat, rye, or barley. Milk, butter, margarine, real cheese, plain yogurt, and vegetable oils, plain fruits, vegetables, meat, seafood, eggs, nuts, beans and legumes, and flours made from them are gluten-free. Fish, chicken, turkey, and beef are gluten free as long as the process of cooking them is not breaded.

Foods made from grains (and grain-like plants) that do not contain harmful gluten include the following: Corn in all forms (corn flour, corn meal, grits, etc.). Rice in all forms, amaranth, buckwheat (kasha), Montina, millet, quinoa, teff, fonio, sorghum, and soy are gluten free. Naturally gluten-free starches are corn, arrowroot, and potato starch. Pasta and Noodles that are gluten-free are brands like Notta Pasta. Quinoa pasta is gluten free (made from quinoa and corn).

FOODS CONTAINING GLUTEN
Wheat starch, wheat bran, wheat germ, couscous, cracked wheat, durum, einkorn, emmer, farina, faro, fu (common in Asian foods), gliadin, graham flour, kamut, matzo, semolina, spelt, barley, bulgur, oats (only those processed in plants that produce gluten-containing grains and may be contaminated), rye, seitan, triticale and Mir (a cross between wheat and rye), veggie burgers (if not specified gluten-free).

For baking, substitute these with flours like buckwheat, corn, millet, rice, sorghum, or quinoa. You'll need xanthan gum or guar gum as a substitute for gluten when baking. Sticking to unprocessed, fresh, whole foods will naturally keep a person's diet gluten-free, as well as help heal the intestinal tract of any existing gluten damage. Typically, most African countries make puff puff, pancakes and patti dough from white flour. I have introduced a couple of recipes for those who want to substitute regular flour with gluten-free alternatives. You can now make puff puff from oatmeal or rice flour or any gluten free flour. You just need to add the right amount of xantham gum.

FISH

Fish is an essential food item in the diet of many people in Africa. Much of the fish consumed in West Africa consists of species such as sardinella, bonga, mackerel, horse mackerel, anchovies, and tilapia. High value fish are exported from the poor, under-nourished countries to the rich nations. Thus, the vast potential of marine fishery resources in West Africa is not contributing much to the alleviation of protein malnutrition, especially in hinterland areas. However, fish exports are economically prudent, as the high value species are generally expensive in the local market and unaffordable to many people.

In the Sahelian zone (Mali, Senegal, Niger, Gambia, and Chad), fermented fish products are very popular as a condiment in traditional meals. Ghanaian consumers often claim that well cured freshwater fish tastes better than marine fish. For this reason, certain freshwater species are highly valued and expensive. Fresh tilapia, smoked catfish, and Nile perch are in high demand by middle and high income groups in the urban centers.

Stockfish is an unsalted fish, especially cod, whitefish, pollock, haddock, or ling, dried by cold air and wind on wooded racks. The generic name "stockfish" probably stems from the Dutch (stokvis) stick fish, which refers to the wooden rack on which the fish is dried. Stockfish has a shelf life of several years. It is a popular fish for soups in Nigeria and Cameroon. It has a very pungent smell, but the finished product is usually mouth-watering. The secret in handling stockfish is soaking the piece that will be used overnight, or for a couple of hours. It is the main ingredient in the Igbo snack called "Ugba na Okporoko." The Igbo tribe of Nigeria refers to stockfish as okporoko, which literally translates to "that which produces in the pot." The Bakweri people from the English-speaking part of Cameroon use stockfish to flavor their palm nut or banga soup, which can then be eaten with a cocoyam pudding called kwacoco.
The Tilapia is a popular fish for grilling in Ghana and Cameroon. The fried or grilled croaker is more commonly eaten with ugali in Kenya, while fried croaker is common in Nigerian stews.

Cameroon is also known for its fish consumption at all levels. It is very common to find local fish grills along road sides between major cities and within the cities. Due to the unique exotic herbs and spices from the forests in Cameroon, the flavor of Cameroonian grilled fish is most sought out by other nationalities. The Cameroonian grilled fish is one of the many food items that a tourist remembers after leaving Cameroon. Unfortunately most of the fish consumed in Cameroon is imported.

BAKED OR GRILLED FISH

Whole tilapia or fish of choice
MammyDoro Seafood Seasoning
Lemon or lime juice
1 roma (plum) tomato
1 small onion
Salt, Maggi, Bouillon, or Knorr cubes to taste
Vegetable oil

Put fish in large bowl and add salt and water. Let sit for at least 30 minutes.
Wash fish properly with lemon or lime juice and rinse. Make cuts on fish (but not too deep) to allow seasoning to seep in. Sprinkle MammyDoro Seafood Seasoning on fish and rub all over. In a small bowl, add ½ cup vegetable oil to two tablespoons full of MammyDoro Seafood Seasoning. Blend tomato and onions with ½ cup of water and add to bowl. Add ½ teaspoon salt, 1 Maggi or Bouillon or Knorr cube and mix properly. Use brush to apply mixture generously on fish.

Let marinate for about 20 minutes—the longer the better.
Heat oven to 400°C. Place fish on greased tray and put in the oven, or place in grill basket and put on the grill. After 10 minutes, turn fish over carefully if cooking in the oven or flip over grill basket. Turn fish and cook the other side when one side is done.

Suggested Serving: Serve with Leeks sauce, stewed pepper sauce, stewed greens, miyondo, fried plantains or Jollof rice.

INGREDIENTS

FINAL DISH

FISH STEW

Serves 6

3 lbs. fresh fish
3 large fresh tomatoes
1 cup chopped onion
2 cups vegetable oil
2 bell peppers (any colors)
½ cup chopped garlic
1 celery stalk
1 habanero pepper (optional)
2 teaspoons MammyDoro Seafood Seasoning
Salt, Maggi, Bouillon, or Knorr cubes to taste

Cut fish into desired sizes, wash with lemon or lime juice, and steep in salt water for 30 minutes. Blend garlic, onions, tomatoes, celery, and pepper (if desired) into fine paste. Remove fish from salt water. Add 2 Maggi or Knorr cubes or 1 Bouillon cube. Add 2 teaspoons of MammyDoro Seafood Seasoning and mix properly. Let it sit for about 20 minutes. Heat vegetable oil on medium heat for about 2 minutes and pour in fish and seasonings.

Cook for about 30 minutes, shaking the pot every 10 minutes from side to side to prevent sticking and burning underneath. Add 1 teaspoon of curry and chopped bell peppers and let simmer for 10 minutes. Remove pot from heat and let the fish stew sit for about 5 minutes before serving.

Suggested Serving: Serve with fried plantains, steamed rice, jollof rice.

INGREDIENTS

FINAL DISH

PAN FRIED SALMON & GREEN BEANS

Serves 4

1 lb. salmon
¼ cup chopped parsley
¼ cup chopped onions
1 teaspoon MammyDoro Seafood Seasoning
1 lb. green beans
¼ cup finely chopped onion
½ teaspoon MammyDoro Vegetable Seasoning
Cooking oil
Salt to taste

Soak salmon in salt water for about 30 minutes. Strain and marinate with Seafood Seasoning and let sit for about 10 minutes. Chop up onion and parsley. Heat up 3 tablespoons of olive oil in non-stick saucepan. Add onion and parsley and stir. Add fish, reduce heat to low, cover the pot, and let simmer for about 5 minutes. Open saucepan and flip fish over. Cover for another 5 minutes; turn off the heat. The steam continues to cook the fish, and it should flake easily when poked with a fork.

Bring 4 cups water to a boil and add a pinch of salt or baking soda. Put the green beans into the boiling water and let cook for 10 minutes. Strain and put beans aside. In a non-stick frying pan, put two tablespoons of vegetable oil or, if oil is left from frying the salmon, you can use it, just add onions. Stir and add ¼ teaspoon MammyDoro Vegetable Seasoning. Add the pre-cooked green beans and continue stirring for about a minute.

Suggested Serving: Serve with green beans, and steamed rice, grilled zucchini or boiled potatoes.

INGREDIENTS

FINAL DISH

FRIED FISH

Whole tilapia or fish of choice
MammyDoro Seafood Seasoning
Lemon or lime juice
2-4 njangsa seeds
1 or 2 roma tomatoes
Salt, Maggi, Bouillon or Knorr cubes to taste
Frying oil

Method

Put fish in large bowl and add salt and water, let soak for at least 30 minutes. Wash fish with lemon or lime juice and rinse. Cut fish into required sizes and place in a bowl. Sprinkle MammyDoro Seafood Seasoning on fish. Add salt, Maggi, Bouillon or Knorr cubes to taste. Grind a few grains of MammyDoro Njangsa Seeds together with 1 or 2 roma tomatoes using ¼ cup of water and pour over the fish. Mix properly and let marinate for about 20 minutes – the longer the better. The oil in the njangsa seeds gives a nice shine to the fish when fried and enhances the flavor of the fish as well.

Heat frying oil and preferably use a shallow frying pan so that the fish is not completely submerged in oil when cooking. Fry one side of the fish for about 5 minutes, flip fish over and fry the other side. Remove and place on a paper towel to remove excess frying oil from fish.

Suggested Serving: Serve with stewed pepper sauce, stewed greens, miyondo, fried plantains, Jollof rice or Ugali.

INGREDIENTS

FINAL DISH

MBONGO TCHOBI

(Blackened Fish Stew) - Serves 6

5 lbs. catfish or fresh fish of your choice
3 teaspoons MammyDoro Mbongo Seasoning
5 roma (plum) tomatoes
5 oz. chopped onions
2 cups vegetable oil
3 oz. garlic pods
2½ oz. Njangsang grains
1 celery stalk
Salt, Maggi, Bouillon, or Knorr cubes to taste
Pepper to taste (optional)

Cut and wash fish with lemon or lime juice, steep in salt water for about 30 minutes, and strain. Add MammyDoro Mbongo Seasoning, salt, Maggi/Bouillon/Knorr cubes, mix properly, and set aside. If njangsa seeds are used, blend separately with a cup of water and sieve over the fish. Peel garlic, put in a blender, and add in chopped onions, tomatoes, and chopped celery. Add pepper (optional) and blend properly into fine puree. Pour pureed herbs into the bowl of seasoned fish and mix.

Heat vegetable oil on medium heat for about 3 minutes and add seasoned fish and herbs into oil. Rinse bowl with a bit of water and add into pot. Shake the pot and allow it to cook for about 30 minutes, shaking the pot from side to side every 10 minutes. Maintain the thickness as desired. Add salt, pepper, and Maggi to taste. Allow to simmer for about 20 minutes on low heat.

Suggested Serving: Serve with steamed rice, boiled or fried plantains, boiled yam or sweet potatoes.

INGREDIENTS

FINAL DISH

FUFU

Fufu is a term used to classify all dough-like substances made from different tubers and crops. The dish is further identified by the name of the tuber or crop from which it is made. Most of countries in West, Central, East, and South Africa eat fufu of some sort. Fufu is a starchy accompaniment to stews and other dishes with sauces. Fufu is to West, Central, East, and South African cooking as mashed potatoes is to the traditional American cooking. Their consistencies, however, are different. The texture of fufu is similar to unbaked bread dough. Traditionally, fufu is made from tubers like yams, cassava, cocoyams, taro, or grains like rice, oatmeal, maize, or a combination of two of the aforementioned products. Fufu from corn (maize) is widely eaten in East Africa (ugali) and (nshima) in Zambia. It is known as nsima in Malawi, sadza in Zimbabwe, pap in South Africa, posho in Uganda, luku, fufu, nshima, moteke, semoule, ugali and bugari in Republic of the Congo and in the Democratic Republic of the Congo and phaletshe in Botswana. West Africans also use corn (maize) to make fufu. In Ghana, maize is used to make banku and kenkey. In Cameroon, Togo, and Benin, it is used to make corn fufu, while in Northern Nigeria it is used to make tuwon masara. In the Congo Basin, fufu is often made from cassava tubers, while Liberians enjoy dumboy (another type of fufu made from cassava flour) and eaten with fish soup.

Fufu is generally eaten at dinner because it requires a lot of time and energy to prep and cook the tuber or grain from which it is made. Fufu from tubers like cocoyams (malanga/taro), yams, cassava (yuca), and plantains is made by first peeling, then washing and boiling the tuber. When done, they are removed one at a time and dropped into a wooden mortar, with two people pounding as the tubers are being dropped from the boiling pot. The tuber must be hot because it is easier to mash when it's hot. In the evenings, the melody from the pounding of fufu fills the air as each household prepares dinner. The traditional method is to boil the tuber and pound them in a wooden mortar until it becomes a smooth and sticky dough. A vast majority of Sub-Saharan Africa eats corn fufu. Up until the early '90s, African immigrants had to improvise fufu by cooking potato flakes or Bisquick. Nowadays, thanks to the industrialization of farming in Nigeria and Ghana, Africans are able to get processed yam, plantain, cocoyam, cassava, and potato flour from African markets abroad. My recommendation is to still cook the tubers and make your own fufu. The process might be quite laborious, but the quality of the food is invaluable. Fresh food is always better since you do not have to deal with any amount of preservatives in some pre-processed flours.

By 2005, the United States of America became the largest producer of ethanol fuel in the world. Historically, most of United States ethanol has come from corn. The effect of commercializing corn was felt in several areas—the corn-fufu eating immigrants not left out. Someone came up with the idea that oatmeal could be used as a substitute for corn since the price of oatmeal was stable and the benefits of eating oatmeal as fufu outweighed the benefits of cornmeal. When I got the news of this substitute, I quickly went on a mission to educate households on the benefits of oatmeal fufu. I subsequently introduced it as a new menu item at Motherland Kitchen. One can rightly say that in terms of taste and benefits, oatmeal fufu is the best. But some people still prefer corn fufu, perhaps because it is hard to break old habits.

Achu (taro mash) is a delicacy in the West and North West regions of Cameroon. This is a mash of taro that is eaten with the palm oil spicy sauce containing lots of variety meats, with boiled eggplants and huckleberry leaves as sides. The consistency of taro mash is like mashed potatoes with the difference just in how sticky it is because taro is less watery than potatoes. To this day, the women in the villages boil and pound the taro root one at a time with a pestle that has a flat head like a wooded spoon. It is amazing how they succeed to make a final product that smooth with such an instrument. As they say, necessity is the mother of invention. Immigrants from Cameroon have found an alternative in the Champion juicer. It produces excellent taro mash in seconds. Is the price of the Champion Juicer too high compared to the need of achu? A used one is about $300. That is an investment that can be justified if the juicer will be used to mass produce achu for a restaurant or a large family that eats achu once or twice a week. There is an alternative: all you need is a walk to the dollar store and some muscle. Taro and potatoes are similar except for the fact that potatoes are softer when cooked. Get a potato masher and enjoy achu at home. It is that simple. I will show you how in this book.

In Ghana, the same taro roots are cooked differently. They are peeled and boiled with salt and black pepper. When they are soft enough to be easily pounded, the water is drained and the taro roots pounded into a thick paste, shaped into balls, and eaten with any soup of choice, preferably the peanut butter soup. The difference with achu is just the consistency: mashed potato-like in Cameroon and dough-like in Ghana, with a little bit of seasoning. Ugali from maize or corn is very popular in the East and South of Africa. Other flours like millet and sorghum are also used to make ugali, but the most popular flour used to make ugali is maize. The texture depends on the individual families. Some families make uguli hard and others make it a bit softer. It is just a matter of preference. Generally in Kenya, ugali is hard and mostly made using the white corn. Yellow or brown corn is also used to make ugali in Tanzania and other East African countries.

ACHU FUFU

(Mashed Taro roots)

3 lbs. taro root
½ cup plantain flour

Equipment
Potato masher
6" open-mouth bowl or pot

Boil taro root for 1 hour or until it is well done and soft. Put cold water in a bowl and set aside. When taro roots are done, turn heat to very low. It is important to keep the pot hot while mashing the root; this makes it easier to mash. Remove the roots one at a time and drop in the small bowl of cold water. Peel off quickly and drop in the pot or bowl and use the potato masher to mash and pound if necessary. Continue the process until all the roots are mashed. If two people are doing this, one person peeling the root and the other mashing, it will be more convenient and go faster.

Continue to mash until mixture is smooth. If the taro roots were too fresh, the mashed taro could be too soft. In that case, measure a ½ cup of plantain flour, add 1½ cups cold water; mix properly. Set the pot on the stove and stir until plantain is cooked. It should take about 5 minutes. Pour mixture into the taro mash and mix with a wooden spoon, pressing and mashing any lumps that were not mashed by the potato masher. Mix properly and serve.

Suggested Serving: Serve with Achu Soup.

INGREDIENTS

FINAL DISH

CASSAVA FUFU

(Frozen cassava – water fufu)

Frozen cassava (yucca)
Rice flour (optional)
Water

To dissolve the frozen cassava, pour hot water over it and mash using your fingers. This helps to break it down and dissolve easily. Add cold water when paste is completely dissolved. Mix properly and make sure there are no lumps in the mixture. Set aside for about 10 minutes for the cassava to separate from the water. Gently drain water, leaving a thick paste at the bottom of the bowl. Pour the paste into a small, deep pot and begin to stir with a wooden spoon. Preferably, use a thick wooden spoon, as cassava fufu tends to thicken very fast. Continue stirring and watching the color change from white to translucent. If for some reason the cassava is cooked and the texture is not firm enough, add 1 tablespoon of rice flour. This helps to bind the cassava fufu. Rice flour is better because it does not change the flavor of the cassava fufu and cooks instantaneously. When done, mold the fufu into desired sizes and serve. Because this fufu is very thick, the sizes are usually smaller than fufu from corn or oatmeal.

Suggested Serving: Serve hot with any sauce of choice.

CORN FUFU

Serves 2

Ugali – Kenya, Tanzania
Nshima – Zambia, Malawi
Pap – South Africa, Namibia
Sadza – Zimbabwe
Tuwon – Northern Nigeria
Kiban – North West Cameroon
Futu – Ivory Coast
Posho – Uganda
Kpekple – Ghana
Bidia – Democratic Republic of Congo

1 cup corn flour
2 cups water

Bring water to a boil in a small pot (about 3 cups). Reduce the water into a small dish leaving 2 cups in the pot Add 1 cup of corn flour into the water. Reduce heat to medium and stir until consistency is stiff. Add ½ cup from reserved hot water, cover, and let the fufu cook for about 5 minutes. Stir again until smooth. If fufu is too stiff, add a little bit of water and continue to stir to desired consistency. Use a saucer or spatula to remove the fufu and put in a bowl. Make sure the bowl is smooth and a little wet to prevent the dough from sticking to the walls of the bowl. Move the fufu in a circular manner to form a smooth mound. Place it on a plate or small bowl. The fufu, when done, will look like thick grits or dough.

Note: If you are planning to make corn fufu for a large number of people, 4 or more, then after boiling the water, mix 1 cup of corn flour in 2 cups cold water, add to 1 cup of boiled water, and stir. Continue to stir for about 10 minutes or until mixture starts to produce bubbles. Add the remainder of corn flour and stir vigorously. The reason for this is to make sure there are no lumps in the fufu. You want the fufu to be very smooth when done.

Suggested Serving: Serve hot with any sauce of choice.

INGREDIENTS

FINAL DISH

OATMEAL FUFU

Serves 2

1 cup oatmeal flour
3 cups water

Bring water to a boil in a small pot or kettle. Reduce the water into a small dish if boiled using a pot. Leave about 1 cup in the pot or pour out 1 cup of water from the kettle into the pot. Add 1 cup of oatmeal flour into the water. Reduce heat to medium and stir until consistency is stiff. Add 1 cup of water, cover, and let the fufu cook for about 5 minutes. Stir again and use a small saucer or spatula to remove the fufu and put in a bowl. Make sure the bowl is smooth and a little wet to prevent the dough from sticking to the walls of the bowl. Move the fufu in a circular manner to form a smooth mound. Place it on a plate or small bowl. The fufu, when done, will look like thick, uncooked dough.

Suggested Serving: Serve hot with any sauce or stew of choice.

INGREDIENTS

FINAL DISH

YAM FUFU

Serves 2

Yam flour
Water

Bring water to a boil in a small pot or kettle (about 2 cups). Reduce the water into a small dish if boiled using a pot. Leave about 1 cup in the pot or pour out 1 cup from the kettle into the pot. Add ½ cup of yam flour into the water. Reduce heat to medium and stir until consistency is stiff. Yam flour is pre-processed, so it does not need extra time to cook. Move the fufu in a circular-clockwise manner to form a smooth mound. If mixture is not perfectly smooth, add a little hot water and stir again. Use a small saucer or spatula to remove the fufu and put in a bowl. Make sure the bowl is smooth and a little wet to prevent the dough from sticking to the walls of the bowl. Place it on a plate or small bowl. When done, yam fufu looks like thick, uncooked dough.

Suggested Serving: Serve hot with any soup or stew of choice.

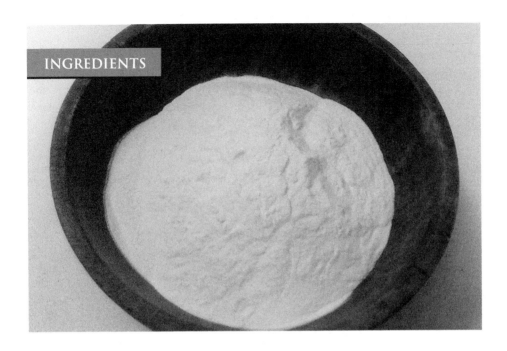

INGREDIENTS

FINAL DISH

MORTAR AND PESTLE

You can still use a mortar and pestle to make you favorite fufu. Freshly made fufu tastes completely different from the fast version made from the processed flours. Treat yourself to a delicious meal of real fufu by making your own pounded yam (poundo), cassava (dumboy), or cocoyam (akwa). You may never go back to cooking the processed flour after you taste the original flavor. All you need is some muscle to pound the fufu.

PLANTAINS

Plantains are a member of the banana family. They look a lot like green bananas when unripe, but they are very different. They are starchy and low in sugar when they are unripe. They must be cooked before serving because they cannot be eaten raw. Plantains are a side dish just like potatoes would be in America or Europe. They are very popular in different forms in Latin America, West Africa, and the Caribbean countries. They are usually fried or baked when they become yellow. They can also be fried or baked when green. They are high in carbohydrates, potassium, and vitamins. Contrary to what those who try to lose weight might think, plantains are very high in carbohydrates and are low in saturated fat and sodium. They are a good source of Vitamin A, Vitamin C, and Vitamin B6. When they become yellow, a large portion of the calories come from the sugars. Dodo/Aloco (Fried Yellow Plantain) is a popular side dish in Nigeria and Cameroon. In Cameroon, the fried plantain is served with grilled fish or "Mbongo tchobi"—blackened fish stew. It is also served as an accompaniment to stewed beans. In Nigeria, dodo is a side to a Jellof rice and stew dish. Aloko is also an Ivorian snack made from deep fried plantains or green bananas that is served as an accompaniment to grilled fish. The other traditional way to eat fried plantains in Ivory Coast is to serve it with fried onions and hot pepper sauce. This combination is not only delicious but also the sugar in the yellow fried plantain helps cool off the heat in the pepper. Ndizi kanga, as they are called in Tanzania, is a very popular food item in urban areas. The Mexican style fried green plantain is also common in Cameroon. It is served with a vegetable dish like Ndole (bitter leaf sauce) or grilled chicken and greens. It is commonly referred to as "plantain tappe" in Cameroon. It is very crunchy and delicious when eaten hot, and it is usually fried either green or halfway ripe. This method is not good with yellow plantains because the pressing process makes the plantains mushy and unpresentable when fried the second time. The sugar in the plantains also makes it look black and foams when deep fried. Whether boiled or fried green, near ripe, or ripe, it is a matter of personal preference. The Metta tribe of the North West Region of Cameroon is noted for their very delicious porridge, cocoyams, or plantains. It is believed that the "Pikin Planti" dish originated from this tribe. Also they produce the best quality palm oil in the region. As a symbol of happiness and gratitude for the new born (pickin), a lot of palm oil is used in making this special dish. The overflow of red palm oil is a sign that the nursing mother is well taken care of by her in-laws. The palm oil saps into the plantain, which is cooked whole, and makes the plantain softer. This, in turn, makes it easy for the nursing mother to chew. It is also noteworthy that the plantain from the North West Region of Cameroon is not usually as soft as those from the other regions.

FRIED YELLOW PLANTAINS

(Dodo / Aloco)

#themotherlandcookbook

1 ripe plantain
Pinch of salt (optional)
Vegetable oil for deep frying

Peel and slice into desired shape. Add a pinch of salt and mix to increase sweetness (optional). Heat vegetable oil for about 15 minutes in a frying pan.
Add plantain slices into hot oil. Fry until the slices are golden brown, flipping each slice to properly cook. Remove with a slotted spoon and set on a paper towel to drain. Repeat until all the plantains have been fried.

Suggested Serving: Serve hot with any meat or vegetable stew, grilled fish, meat, chicken and hot sauce.

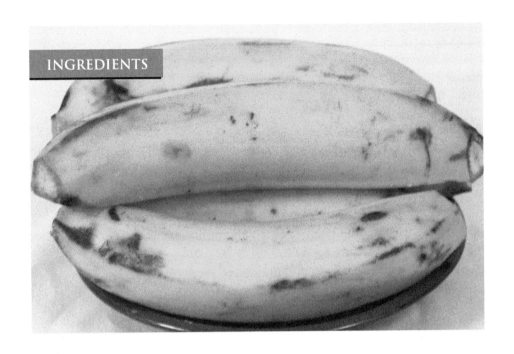

INGREDIENTS

FINAL DISH

FRIED GREEN PLANTAINS

(Plantain tappe)

1 green plantain
Vegetable oil (for deep-frying)

Cut plantain into two halves. Heat vegetable oil for about 15 minutes in a frying pot. Add plantain pieces into hot oil. Fry until the pieces are golden brown. Remove with a slotted spoon and set on a wood board. Use rolling pin to flatten and drop flattened plantain back into oil to let the inside cook. Fry for 5 minutes and remove. Place on paper towel to drain.

Suggested Serving: Serve hot because green plantains harden faster than yellow plantains when cold. Serve with vegetables, grilled fish, chicken or meat.

INGREDIENTS

FINAL DISH

PORRIDGE

Porridge by definition is a breakfast dish usually served hot made from a grain and cooked in milk or water. Other legumes or fruits, nuts, sugar, or honey could be added to give the dish a savoury taste or sweetness. There are different varieties of porridge on the continent of Africa. This s simply because the grain used in various regions depends on what is commonly grown. In northern Africa, porridge is mostly from barley while millet and sorghum are used in Sub-Saharan Africa. From the West Coast to the East and South of Africa, corn is commonly used. These dishes are similar to the American grits, but lighter in texture since the flours are not as coarse as grits or oatmeal. No butter is added to it. Some people add sugar and milk or sour cream, while others add limes to their porridge. In Cameroon and Nigeria, this porridge is called pap, akamu, or ogi. In Tanzania it is referred to as uji.

In this chapter, however, the term Porridge will be used to refer to dishes with a soupy texture. These would be similar to the Western corn chowder soup, bean soup, etc. The difference is that these soups in Africa would include chunks of meat and or fish and either yams, potatoes, plantains, cocoyams, or cassava. This terminology is interpreted and understood differently from one African country to the other. Cassava porridge (Ebe) is typically eaten in Sierra Leone and Gambia. It is a simple dish that has a sweet and sour taste, with a rich fish flavor from the dry fish, fresh shrimps, and limes. It is very spicy and also eaten by their neighbors from Senegal. Cocoyam porridge is popular in the West and Northwestern regions of Cameroon. It is also very easy to make and requires very few ingredients. The basic ingredients are the crayfish and palm oil, together with peppers and smoked fish of choice. Some tribes like "Metta" of the North West region of Cameroon add bitter leaf to the porridge. Ekpwang coco is one of the delicacies of Cameroon and South Eastern Nigeria. The cocoyams in the US are different from those in Africa. Some workaround can be done to get the same results in terms of texture by using both the red and white cocoyams to prepare ekpwang coco. The red is a little too dry and the white is too soft, so the best texture will be a blend of the two. The leaf of choice is cocoyam, which you may use if you like. However, I have great results with turnip green leaves, which also happen to be quite affordable. Some regions in Nigeria prepare this dish with yams instead of cocoyams. Yams are more easily available than cocoyams. Cameroon's Sese plantain is a common pick-me-up dish in the evening, especially when it is cold. It is cooked in soup form, which emphasizes the stock and not the meat or plantains that are used to make the dish. It is therefore important that the ingredients are enough and standout to give that needed boost that the eater is looking for. It is also usually spicy. Typically crayfish, smoked fish, herbs, and spices are enough to give the much-needed flavor.

Meat is not necessarily required to make this dish.

"Pickin" is the common name for a precious new born. Traditionally, a special day is set aside for the welcoming and thanksgiving to honor this bundle of joy. This day has nothing to do with the Naming Ceremony or the Christening. It is just a day of Thanksgiving. It is a day to acknowledge abundance of blessings. Accordingly, there is an abundance of oil used in preparing this dish called "Pickin Planti." It is expected that the guests will follow the flowing of the oil with their tongues, as it spills on their fingers and runs down their hands, which makes for a tasty experience. Potato hot pot is a very simple and delicious dish that is commonly cooked in the South West and North West regions of Cameroon. It is most popular in the North West Region because that is where potatoes are grown. It is such an abundant commodity that everyone can afford to have it for breakfast, lunch, or dinner. The Potato hot pot is also commonly served during celebrations due to its relative cost as compared to other dishes whose ingredients will require a lot more money to purchase. It is also a very colorful dish, as carrots, green beans, and bell peppers are included. When made with chicken, it has the look of Chicken DG but the difference is the extra soup that comes with the Potato hot pot due to the consistency of cooked potatoes, which makes it easy to become a porridge.

Yam Porridge is typically cooked in Nigeria and Ghana, where yam is one of the main cash and subsistent crops. It is not a common dish in Cameroon, even though there are other species of yam present in the country. The white yams that are similar to those grown in Nigeria and Ghana are also grown in the South West Region of Cameroon. The yellow yam is typically grown in the North West region and has a little bit of a bitter taste, which makes for a good porridge. These types of yams are expensive, and only those who can afford them can enjoy a dish of yam porridge. Optionally, beans are added to the yam porridge to provide the balance of carbohydrates and proteins in the dish.

EBE

(Cassava Porridge) - Serves 10   #themotherlandcookbook

4 lbs. cassava (yucca)
5 bonny dry fish
1 lb. shrimps
1 lb. crab legs
½ cup ground crayfish
1 cup chopped onions
2 habanero peppers (optional)
6 limes
2 cups palm oil
1 teaspoon MammyDoro Porridge Seasoning
Enough water to make the soup
Sea salt, Maggi, Bouillon, or Knorr cubes to taste

Soak bonny fish for at least 30 minutes. Put 15 cups water into a large pot. Add cassava and salt to taste. Cook for about 20 minutes; add crab legs, Maggi, and palm oil. Blend onions, add to pot, and continue to cook for another 20 minutes. Remove bones from bonny fish, put into the blender together with the crayfish and pepper. Blend into a fine paste and pour into the pot. Wash and add shrimps into the soup and continue to cook until cassava is well done. The cassava should be properly cooked to act as thickener to the porridge. If too thick, add a cup or two of water.
When cassava is well done, pour out stock into a large bowl. Squeeze the lime into the stock. Measure stock two cups at a time and blend. This should change the stock into a thick, yellow color, evenly distributed. Pour the stock back into the pot. Continue process until all the stock is properly mixed. Taste and adjust seasonings as needed.

Suggested Serving: Serve warm.

INGREDIENTS

FINAL DISH

EKPWANG COCO

(Grated Cocoyam Porridge) - Serves 8

4 red and 4 white cocoyams
1 cup chopped onions
2 habanero peppers (optional)
3 bundles of fresh turnip leaves
1 cup mixed parsley, basil, cilantro
2 teaspoons MammyDoro Porridge Seasoning
6 dry bonny fish and 1 piece kutta or kini fish

Salt, Maggi, Bouillon, or Knorr cubes to taste
3 roma (plum) tomatoes
1 cup chopped leeks
1 cup crayfish
2 cups palm oil
10 cups water
½ cup chopped ginger
1 lb. of beef

Soak bonny fish in cold water for about 2 hours and remove bones. Wash and cut up meat into bite sizes. Add to pot. Add 1 teaspoon of salt, 2 Maggi or Knorr cubes. Blend onions, leeks, tomatoes, parsley, basil, cilantro, and ginger and add to meat. Add pre-soaked bonny fish to pot and 2 teaspoons of MammyDoro Porridge Seasoning. Add 6 cups water and cook until tender. Set aside. Grate cocoyam, alternating between red and white to facilitate mixing. Add 1 teaspoon of salt when done and mix thoroughly. Set aside. Grind crayfish and set aside.

In another larger, non-stick pot: Oil bottom and sides of pot with 1 cup of palm oil. Wash turnip leaves and gently pull leaves from stem, cutting them large enough to wrap a teaspoonful of grated cocoyam without spilling at ends. Preserve smaller leaves to chop and cook with another dish. Start wrapping grated cocoyam and placing the wrapped ekpwang in a crisscross manner to allow for easy circulation of water between the ekpwang when cooking. While wrapping the ekpwang, bring 4 cups water to a boil in a kettle. When done wrapping, put the pot on the stove, pour in boiling water. Add crayfish. Cook for 15 minutes on high heat. Reduce heat to medium. Use wooden spoon to stir around the pot. Lift pot and shake from side to side, causing the ekpwang to mix up. Add pepper if desired. Add pre-cooked meat and palm oil and cook for 1 hour. Check to make sure water is not drying up. If you need a lot of sauce, add more hot water as needed. Taste for seasoning and adjust as needed.

Suggested Serving: Serve warm.

INGREDIENTS

FINAL DISH

PICKIN PLANTI

(Special Plantain Porridge) - Serves 10

10 green plantains
5 bonny dry fish
2 lbs. beef bones or neck bones
1 cup ground crayfish
1 large onion and 1 whole leek
3 habanero peppers (optional)
½ cup chopped fresh thyme
2 teaspoons MammyDoro All-Purpose Seasoning
2 teaspoons MammyDoro Porridge Seasoning
Salt, Maggi, Bouillon, or Knorr cubes to taste
2 lbs. cow feet
2 lbs. smoked turkey
1 cup chopped basil
½ gallon of red palm oil
1 cup chopped parsley

Blend ginger, leeks, onions, parsley, basil, thyme, and garlic and set aside. Put cow feet in a pot and add ½ cup of kanwa or nihkiy, 1 teaspoon salt, and enough water to cook the meat. Cook for 30 minutes and add tripe. Continue to cook for another 20 minutes. Add smoked turkey and beef bone or neck bones. Continue to cook for another 20 minutes. Pour palm oil into another larger pot and heat for about 2 minutes—do not bleach. Add crayfish and add the remainder of the blended herbs. Stir for 15 minutes. Add 2 teaspoon MammyDoro Porridge Seasoning and continue to stir for about 15 minutes.

Peel and slice plantains in half, add to pot, and mix. Add water and let cook for about 45 minutes. Then add pre-cooked meat into pot. Add water to desired thickness. Add fresh pepper (whole) and cover the pot. Let cook for another 45 minutes or until plantains are soft and water dries off, leaving just a sauce and clear palm oil. Optionally you may add any green leafy vegetable of choice.

Suggested Serving: Serve warm.

INGREDIENTS

FINAL DISH

POTATO HOT POT

Serves 6

1 lb. chicken
1 cup chopped onions
1 lb. cut green beans
16 oz. tomato sauce
3 lbs. potatoes (preferably red)
1 habanero pepper (optional)
½ red, ½ green, ½ yellow bell pepper
1 cup chopped leeks or green onions
1 cup mixed chopped cilantro, parsley, and basil
2 teaspoons MammyDoro Chicken Seasoning
1 teaspoon MammyDoro Vegetable Seasoning
Salt, Maggi, Bouillon, or Knorr cubes to taste
3 cloves of garlic
1 lb. cut carrots
3 oz. tomato paste
2 cups vegetable oil

Blend garlic, basil, parsley, basil, leeks, or green onions and put aside. Cut carrots and green beans and set aside. Peel potatoes and set aside. If large potatoes are used, peel and cube as needed. Chop tomatoes and onions and set aside. Take skin off of chicken, wash, and cut into bite sizes. Put 1 cup vegetable oil in a saucepan and heat for about 1 minute. Put chicken into pot, add 1 teaspoon salt, and 1 Maggi or Knorr cube or ½ Bouillon cube. Add 2 teaspoons of MammyDoro Chicken Seasoning and chopped onions and mix properly. Continue to stir for 10 minutes. Remove and set aside. Add blended herbs into remaining oil; add tomato paste and ½ cup cooking oil if needed. Stir for 10 minutes; add habanero pepper, tomato sauce, and 6 cups water. Cook for 35 minutes. Add carrots, green beans, potatoes, and pre-cooked chicken. Adjust seasoning to taste and let cook for 5 minutes. Add chopped bell peppers and continue to cook for another 10 minutes.

Suggested Serving: Serve hot.

INGREDIENTS

FINAL DISH

A BOOK OF RECIPES, NUTRITIONAL INFORMATION & EDUCATION

YAM PORRIDGE

Serves 6

4 lbs. yam tubers
4 bonny dry fish
2 lbs. smoked turkey
2 lbs. beef neck bones
1 cup ground crayfish
1 large onion
1 cup chopped leeks
1 habanero pepper (or more)
½ cup chopped parsley
½ cup chopped basil
½ cup fresh thyme
1 cup palm oil
1 teaspoon MammyDoro Porridge Seasoning
Sea salt, Maggi, Bouillon, or Knorr cubes to taste

Blend ginger, leeks, onions, thyme, and garlic and set aside. Soak bonny fish and/or smoked fish in water for about 30 minutes. Remove bones and shred. Pour palm oil into a saucepan and heat for about 2 minutes. Add crayfish and stir. Add shredded pre-soaked dry fish and blended herbs. Add ½ teaspoon salt, 1 Maggi or Knorr cube or ½ Bouillon cube. Wash and add beef bones, smoked turkey, and enough water to cook the meat. Cook for about 45 minutes. Peel and cube yam into desired sizes, add to pot, and mix. Add 1 teaspoon MammyDoro Porridge Seasoning and pepper, if desired, and stir. Let cook for another 20 minutes or until yams are soft. Taste and adjust seasoning as needed.

Suggested Serving: Serve hot.

INGREDIENTS

FINAL DISH

CASSAVA (YUCA)

Cassava is the third largest source of food carbohydrates in the tropics, after rice and corn (maize). It is a major staple food in Africa, and other parts of the developing world, providing a basic diet for over half a billion people. It is one of the most drought-tolerant crops, capable of growing on marginal soils. It contains fewer carbohydrates than rice and corn. Nigeria is the world's largest producer of cassava. Cassava leaves are a good source of protein (lysine). It is, however, noteworthy that there are two types of leaves: the edible and the non-edible types of cassava leaves.

Edible Leaf   *Non-Edible Leaf*

Cassava is classified as sweet or bitter. So, too, are the leaves. The sweet leaves are those that are used in making cassava leaf sauce. They may contain some amount of cyanide (toxin), so it is important to make sure that the leaves are from the "sweet" cassava roots because the amount of cyanide will be minimal. Countries that grow mostly bitter cassava roots do not cook the cassava leaf. These countries only process the cassava root as a source of carbohydrates because the leaves are bitter as well and contain a considerable amount of cyanide. It is always advisable to know the source of your cassava and cassava products as well as the cassava leaf. Some producers understand the risks in eating cassava products with high amounts of cyanide and will ferment the cassava for longer periods of time and fry the gari properly. Others do not take that time because of the need to process quickly and sell to make some money. Know your source of gari and cassava products and take note of any changes, such as itchy eyes, dizziness, or headaches after eating cassava products. These are all symptoms of high concentrations of cyanide in the products. I know for sure that the edible cassava leaf is grown in the Center Region (Yaounde) and the North West Region (Djottin) in Cameroon. It is sliced, pounded, dried and crushed, and shipped abroad. It is also pounded, packaged, and shipped frozen. Transporting dried cassava leaf is effortless and I, therefore, prefer and use the dried leaves. The recipe in this book shows how to cook dried, crushed edible cassava leaf. The difference is in the timing; it takes longer for the dried leaves to cook. I add chopped spinach to cassava leaves to make the dry leaves softer and cook faster.

"POULET DG"
CHICKEN DIRECTOR GENERAL

In the late '70s and early '80s, the economy of Cameroon was booming, spurred by the green revolution introduced by Cameroon's first President, El Hadj Amadou Ahidjo, R.I.P. The Agricultural sector was responsible for most of the growth in the economy. As a result, there was money in the hands of citizens to spend, and many small businesses sprung up.

Run primarily by women, a business known as the Chicken Parlor emerged in cities and, later, smaller versions sprung up in towns and villages. These parlors were usually located in the living rooms of the women who owned the business, where mostly chicken dishes and grilled fish were sold. The most striking dish served was "Poulet DG," which translates to "Chicken Director General." The reason this name was given is because Director Generals of State Owned corporations were paid well enough to afford a plate of food for CFAF 5,000, which at the time was 10USD. This is one of the most flavorful and colorful Cameroonian dishes. It is a combination of chicken, bush pepper, a specie of cobeb pepper that grows only in Cameroon, white pepper, carrots, string beans, bell peppers, and half-ripe plantains.

With my experience as a Chef at Motherland Kitchen, I came across people who loved the combination but were either pescetarian or vegetarian. Therefore, I came up with variations of the original "Poulet DG," to satisfy a cross section of people. This section provides recipes for Chicken "Poulet DG," Seafood DG, Beef DG, and Veggie DG.

Beef DG and chicken DG are prepared in the same way because beef and chicken have to be properly cooked before adding the vegetables. On the other hand, veggie DG is quick and simple. Only minimal time is needed to fry the tomato sauce so that the acidity of the tomatoes is reduced. Fish DG is the quickest because fish takes less time to cook; however, it is important to marinate the fish properly. For best results, the fish should be marinated for a long time or overnight.

CHICKEN DG

Serves 6

3 lbs. chicken
6 plantains (green or medium ripe)
½ cup mixed chopped garlic, ginger,
1 cup chopped mixed onions, leeks, parsley, and basil
1 each green, red, yellow bell peppers
1 cup vegetable oil
1 teaspoon MammyDoro Chicken Seasoning
Salt, Maggi, Bouillon, or Knorr cubes to taste
Frying oil for plantains

Blend ginger, garlic, basil, parsley, onions, leeks, and basil and put aside. Cube bell peppers and put aside. Slice and boil carrots and green beans in separate pot and when cooked, strain and put aside. Take skin off of chicken, wash, and cut into bite sizes. Add 2 teaspoons of MammyDoro Chicken Seasoning and mix properly. Put vegetable oil in pot and heat for about 2 minutes. Put chicken in a pot, add salt and Maggi, and stir properly for 5 minutes (no water added). Add blended herbs, adjust seasonings to taste, and let cook for about 25 minutes.

While chicken is cooking:
Slice and fry plantains and put in a bowl over paper napkin to soak off oil.
When chicken is well done, add cut bell peppers to chicken and mix. Let simmer for about 5 minutes. Add boiled carrots and green beans and mix. Add fried plantains in the chicken and mix.

Suggested Serving: Serve as is or accompanied with rice.

SEAFOOD DG

(Plantains) - Serves 2

½ lb. Salmon or fish fillet of choice
½ lb. salmon or fish fillet of choice
½ lb. shrimps (raw preferable)
1 cup vegetable oil (preferably olive oil)
2 plantains (ripe or medium ripe)
3 oz. chopped onions
3 oz. chopped leeks
6 oz. green beans
6 oz. chopped carrots
1 teaspoon MammyDoro Seafood Seasoning
6 oz. green, red, yellow bell peppers
Salt, Maggi, Bouillon, or Knorr cubes to taste

Cut salmon into small pieces, as desired. Clean the shrimps if raw shrimps are used. In a large bowl, add cold water and salt, and steep the fish in it for about 10 minutes, then strain. Add 1 teaspoon of MammyDoro Seafood Seasoning, salt, and Maggi, Bouillon, or Knorr cubes. Mix properly.

Put vegetable oil into pot and heat for 1 minute. Add chopped onions and leeks into the heated oil and stir. Add salmon and shrimps (if raw). Add chopped bell peppers, cover saucepan, and let simmer for about 3 minutes, then open and flip the salmon pieces.

While fish is cooking, boil mixed vegetables in a separate pot and strain. Slice and fry plantains. If rice is preferred, boil the rice. Strain and add boiled mixed vegetables and stir carefully for 3 minutes. Add fried plantains in the mixture and serve.

Suggested Serving: Serve with fried plantains or steamed rice.

INGREDIENTS

FINAL DISH

SEAFOOD DG

(Quinoa Pasta) - Serves 4

½ lb. salmon or fish fillet of choice
½ lb. shrimps (raw preferable)
1 cup vegetable oil (preferably olive oil)
8 oz. quinoa pasta
1 cup chopped onions
½ cup chopped leeks
2 cups cut green beans
2 cups sliced carrots
1 teaspoon MammyDoro Seafood Seasoning
6 oz. green, red, yellow bell peppers
Sea salt, Maggi, Bouillon, or Knorr cubes to taste

Cut salmon into small pieces, as desired. Clean the shrimps if raw shrimps are used and add to salmon. Rinse and add to a bowl. Add 1 teaspoon of MammyDoro Seafood Seasoning, ½ teaspoon of salt, 1 Maggi, Bouillon, or Knorr cube, and mix properly.

Put vegetable oil into pot and heat for 1 minute. Add chopped onions and leeks into the heated oil and stir. Add salmon and shrimps (if raw). Add chopped bell peppers, cover saucepan, and let simmer for about 3 minutes, then open and flip the salmon pieces. While fish is cooking, put water in a large pot and bring to a boil. Add quinoa pasta and a pinch of salt. Cook for 1 minute and add mixed vegetables. Continue to cook for another 5 minutes. Strain and put aside. When salmon and shrimps are well done, add boiled mixed vegetables and quinoa pasta and stir carefully for 3 minutes. Taste and adjust seasonings as needed.

Suggested Serving: Serve warm.

INGREDIENTS

FINAL DISH

VEGGIE DG

Serves 6

1 cup vegetable oil (preferably olive oil)
1 cup chopped onion
1 cup chopped mixed basil, parsley, and cilantro
1 cup mixed red, green, yellow bell peppers
1 cup chopped leeks or green onions
2 roma (plum) tomatoes
1 tablespoon tomato paste
1 lb. each of carrots, green beans, lima beans, zucchini, squash, broccoli
2 teaspoons MammyDoro Vegetable Seasoning
Salt, Maggi, Bouillon, or Knorr cubes to taste

Finely chop up onions and leeks and put aside. Blend basil, parsley, cilantro with half cup of water and put aside. Wash, cut tomatoes in half, squeeze out seeds, chop up, and put aside. Wash, de-seed, and chop up bell peppers and put aside.

In a large pot, bring water to a boil; add 1 teaspoon of salt, carrots, green beans, lima beans, zucchini, squash, and let cook for 10 minutes. Then use a slotted spoon to remove the vegetables, put in a bowl, and set aside. Add the chopped broccoli into the stock and let sit for 10 minutes before straining.

Put vegetable oil into the pot and heat for 2 minutes on high heat, then reduce the heat to medium. Add tomato paste, chopped onions, and leeks or green onions into the heated oil. Stir for 5 minutes and add chopped tomatoes. Add 1 teaspoon salt, 2 Maggi or Knorr cubes, and stir for about 5 minutes. Add one teaspoon of MammyDoro Vegetable Seasoning and continue to stir for another 5 minutes. Add two cups water. Continue to cook for 30 minutes on medium heat. Add mixed vegetables, chopped bell peppers, and let simmer for about 5 minutes. Add broccoli and mix. Take pot off stove to prevent over-cooking of vegetables.

Suggested Serving: Serve with steamed rice, fried plantains, boiled potatoes or yams.

INGREDIENTS

FINAL DISH

PUDDINGS

The term "pudding" in Cameroon refers to dishes that do not at all resemble Western puddings. These are made from sweet corn, pumpkin seeds, groundnuts, black-eyed peas, etc. These dishes taste completely different and wonderful when they are made using banana leaves, which can be purchased from Asian food stores. But you must be an expert in using them because there is a possibility of spilling or even boring holes that will be noticed only when the pot starts to boil. A safer cooking method is to use aluminum foil or vegetable steam bags. The finished product molds into whatever form the container is in when it is cooked. I use the leaves together with the foil to get both the unique flavor as well as prevent water from getting into the pudding when steaming.

In the early '60s and '70s, Moin Moin was made using tomato paste cans and palm oil. Today, there are various methods of cooking Moin Moin, and the seasonings also differ depending on the cook. One thing is certain: Moin Moin is a delicacy in Nigeria. It is eaten in the afternoons with soaked garri, bread, or just by itself. It is also served as a side in restaurants and as an item in events, such as naming ceremonies, christenings, and weddings. During the harvest season in the grass fields of Cameroon, there is so much corn that the women preserve it for later use. Drying the corn is usually the only option. The immediate use is making fresh corn porridge, which is usually without sugar since it is assumed that the fresh corn is sweet enough. Another option is making a pudding. The fresh cut sweet corn, together with fresh cocoyam leaves or spinach, are combined to make koki corn. During the harvest months, which are September through November, koki corn is a popular dish in the grassfields of Cameroon, where corn is mostly grown.

"Koki beans" is similar to Moin Moin. The only difference is that whereas Moin Moin can be made with either palm or vegetable oil, koki beans can only be made with palm oil. No crayfish, eggs, corned beef, or red bell peppers are added to koki beans. "Koki beans" is a simpler version of Moin Moin. It just requires a lot of palm oil, and onions are optional.

Pumpkin seeds are an excellent source of iron. Pumpkin seeds are a good source of mineral zinc, protein, a variety of antioxidants, and mineral supplements in a wide variety of forms. Their low glycemic index also makes them a healthy choice. Pumpkin seeds have been treasured for years because of their dietary and medicinal benefits. They are typically used in the United States as a snack or in salads, while in Africa they are used as thickener in a stew called Egusi Soup. It is one of the staple dishes of the ordinary household in Nigeria. In Cameroon, pumpkin seeds are generally added to a vegetable dish or used to make a pumpkin seed pudding, which is a delicacy served at special events like weddings because pumpkin seeds (egusi) are not cheap. Do not let the price of white pumpkin seeds or scarcity prevent you from enjoying egusi pudding or egusi soup. You can readily find pumpkin seeds in your grocery store. The color is green, but a little effort to wash them will remove the green coating and you are left with white egusi that tastes just as good as the one found in Africa.

Pumpkin seed pudding is a typical Cameroonian dish. Because pumpkin seeds are expensive and the dish itself requires a lot of condiments, it is not commonly made in households. It is, however, made and sold in beer parlors or restaurants. Pumpkin seed pudding is usually a pass item in weddings and important ceremonies in Cameroon.

Groundnut Mboh is a pudding made from roasted groundnuts. It is usually eaten with tubers like cassava or with bread. It is usually very spicy as well and contains crayfish and any kind of smoked fish.

Kwacoco bible is a typical dish of the Bakweri tribe located at the foot of the Mt. Cameroon in Buea. It is made from grated cocoyams, fish, crayfish, palm oil, and seasonings. Everything is mixed up and steamed cooked, which may explain the pseudo-name 'Bible'.

Mukimo (Moh-Kee-Moh) is a popular dish of the Swahili Village. It is a balanced one-pot dish from central Kenya. It derives its name from the word "kima," meaning "mash" (it often looks like green mashed potatoes). Each of the ingredients enhances the other, making this a dish bursting with flavor. This traditional Kikuyu dish is served at all major ceremonies, especially weddings, funerals, and fundraisers. A celebration is incomplete without this delicacy. It is made with potatoes, corn, peas, and onions and is considered a one-dish meal that possesses most of your daily nutritional requirements.

Tooh-kooni (chuhteu) is a popular dish in the North West region of Cameroon. It is made from potatoes and beans. This dish is commonly found on the menu of most homes during the harvest season. This is because corn, which is a predominant crop in this area, is unavailable for fufu during this season. This delicacy replaces fufu for most families until corn is dried and can be processed for fufu. Tooh-kooni's flavor is enhanced using "country onion," which is only found in the rain forests of Cameroon and Gabon.

EGUSI PUDDING

(Pumpkin Seed) - Serves 4

6 cups egusi (pumpkin seeds)
1 cup crayfish
½ lb. meat of choice
4 oz. smoked fish (bony or catfish and stock fish)
1 cup chopped onions
½ cup chopped ginger
2 teaspoon white pepper
2 habanero peppers (optional)
1 egg
4 cups water
Sea salt, Maggi, Bouillon, or Knorr cubes

Wash and dry your pumpkin seeds if green pumpkin seeds are used. Grind the pumpkin seeds using 4 cups water if seeds are used. If ground pumpkin seeds are used, mix with 4 cups water; the stock from the cooked meat should count as part of the water measured. Soak smoked fish in warm water. Slice meat into very thin slices and put into pot with enough water to cook meat. Blend onions, ginger, and pepper and add to meat. Add shredded smoked fish to meat and cook until well done.

When done, let cool and pour stock into a clean bowl. Beat egg and add to the ground pumpkin seeds. Mix thoroughly, adding stock a cup at a time and watching consistency. Mixture should be fluffy. Grind and add crayfish, and taste for salt and Maggi/Bouillon/Knorr cubes. Add pre-cooked meat and smoked fish and mix properly. Wrap in leaves and/or aluminum foil and steam cook for 2 hours.

Suggested Serving: Let cool, slice and serve as a pass item at cocktails or as filling for your sandwich.

INGREDIENTS

FINAL DISH

GROUNDNUT MBOH

(Peanut Pudding) - Serves 4

2 cups raw peanuts
1 onion, finely chopped
½ cup crayfish
½ teaspoon salt
1 Maggi or Knorr cube
1 habanero pepper
4 bony smoked fish (sardines)

Soak smoked fish for about 2 hours. Shred and add 1 cup of water and chopped onions and cook for 30 minutes and set aside. Fry the groundnuts until they are very brown and then let them cool. Peel off the shell and grind using a dry grinder. No water should be added when grinding. Pour into a non-stick pot and add salt, Maggi or Knorr cube and 1 cup of water and mix properly. Add to the pre-cooked fish and onions. Mix properly and put on the stove and continue mixing. Add crayfish and pepper to taste and continue stirring until water dries off and you can see just the oil from the groundnuts. Take pot off the stove and begin to wrap mixture in banana leaves. Steam cook for 30 minutes and serve.

Note: alternatively you can buy ground roasted peanuts from your grocery store. This will save you the time and trouble of frying or roasting and grinding the peanuts.

Suggested Serving: Serve warm with bread or baked cassava, yam or potato.

INGREDIENTS

FINAL DISH

KOKI BEANS

(Black-eyed peas) - Serves 8

6 cups peeled black-eyed peas or koki beans
1 large onion
1 lb. fresh leaf spinach
16 oz. palm oil
2 fresh peppers (optional)
6 cups water
2 teaspoons of akanwa/potash
Salt, Maggi, Bouillon, or Knorr cubes to taste

Soak black-eyed peas overnight for ease of washing and better cooking. If time is an issue, immediately soak and pass through the blender just enough to crack the beans. Rinse off the black eyes and the skin and soak for as long as possible—the longer the better. Dissolve akanwa in a bowl with 4 cups water and put on the side. Chop up onions and add to the pre-washed beans. If fresh peppers are used, slice and add to beans. Scoop beans 2 cups at a time and add 1 cup of water containing akanwa. Blend until mixture is completely smooth and fluffy
Continue to blend until all beans are blended. Stir vigorously. Warm up palm oil and add to blended beans. Add salt to taste. Add chopped fresh leaf spinach. To get original flavor without the hassle of tying with leaves, cut aluminum foil and place the banana leaf in the center. Pour mixture 1 cup or 2 cups at a time and wrap, making sure foil covers the leaf completely to prevent water from getting into the mixture. Wrap properly and steam-cook for 2 hours.

Suggested Serving: Slice and serve warm or hot with boiled plantains.

INGREDIENTS

FINAL DISH

KOKI CORN

(Vegetarian) - Serves 4

5 cups cut sweet yellow corn
1 lb. yellow corn meal or farina
½ cup chopped onion
1 lb. chopped spinach
1 cup of palm oil
1 teaspoon salt
3½ cups water
1 fresh pepper (optional)
Aluminum foil and/or banana leaves for wrapping

Use 1 cup of water to grind onions (and pepper, if used) to as fine as desired and set aside. Grind corn at 2 cup intervals with 1½ cup of water while making sure corn is not completely ground. Mixture should not be like a smoothie; it should be more like orange juice with pulp. Pour blended corn into a larger bowl and repeat the process until all corn is ground. Add ground onion into the bowl. Once all corn is ground, add yellow corn meal or farina to mixture for binding. Add chopped spinach and mix properly, ensuring proper distribution of spinach and corn meal. Add palm oil for color and flavor and mix properly. Wrap 1 or 2 cups mixture in heavy duty aluminum foil in desired sizes. Use vegetable steam cooking plastic bags to cook koki corn for convenience. Steam cook for 1½ - 2 hours.

Suggested Serving: Let cool and solidify, slice and serve warm.

INGREDIENTS

FINAL DISH

KWACOCO BIBLE

Serves 12

5 lbs. white & red Cocoyam
5 bonny fish
1 kini or catfish (smoked)
1 bunch turnip green
Maggi and salt to taste
Plantain leaves
MammyDoro African Basil
(masepo/nchanwu)

1 cup of palm oil
½ cup of ground crayfish
½ cup nja nja moto (anchovies)
Aluminum foil
Habanero Pepper to taste

Soak bonny fish and smoked fish for at least 3 hours, remove bones, shred into thin pieces, and set aside. Peel, wash, and grate cocoyam alternating between the red and white roots for proper mixing after grating. Add salt, Maggi, pepper, ground crayfish, smoked fish, 1 teaspoon MammyDoro African Basil and 1 teaspoon MammyDoro Porridge Seasoning into grated cocoyam. Mix properly with a wooden spoon. Add shredded turnip green leaves and palm oil; mix and distribute evenly in the paste. Warm banana leaves over stove top or flame, making sure they do not burn. Watch the leaves turn into deep green as you move them over the flame or heat. Cut the leaves into desired sizes, wash, and set aside. Cut the aluminum foil into sizes slightly larger than the banana leave pieces you have cut. Place the leave length-wise on each foil and pour ½ cup of mixed cocoyam paste on the leaf. Arrange the paste length-wise and fold over, like rolling a diploma. Bend both ends of the leaf inwards about an inch from the ends and repeat the process using the foil paper underneath the leaf. Twist both ends of the foil when done wrapping. This helps to prevent steam from entering the leaf while cooking the kwacoco bible. Place the kwacoco bible in a steam pot and cook over medium to high heat for 1hr 30 minutes, checking every 30 minutes to make sure there is enough water to continue steaming. Water tends to evaporate very fast when cooking on high heat. Add more water as needed to completely cook the kwacoco bible. When done, take pot off the stove, unwrap the kwacoco bible, and serve.

Suggested Serving: Serve hot with any sauce of choice.

MOIN MOIN

(Pescetarian)

6 cups black-eyed peas
1 cup chopped onion
1 large red bell pepper
1 cup chopped green onions
2 cups vegetable oil
3 cans tuna fish or corned beef (optional)
1 fresh pepper (optional)
6 cups water
2 teaspoons of Akanwa (limestone) or ½ cup Nihkiy
8 vegetable steam bags or any containers for steaming
Salt, Maggi, Bouillon, or Knorr cubes to taste

For best results and faster cooking, soak peas overnight. If un-cracked black-eyed peas are used, for every two cups water you put in the blender, add one cup of black-eyed peas. Set blender on high and blend for 5 seconds. The idea is to crack the peas, not to blend; this makes for easy washing later on. Soak for a couple of hours or overnight. Wash thoroughly and make sure all black eyes are picked out. Drain water completely and add chopped red peppers, onions, and green onions. Add akanwa or nihkiy to water in a bowl to use for grinding; it softens and takes gas out of the peas. Mix and scoop 2 - 3 cups at a time for blending. Add 1 cup of water each time and blend until soft. Pour blended mixture into another large bowl. When done blending, add salt, Maggi, Bouillon, or Knorr and vegetable oil to mixture. Mix briskly for about 1 minute. Open tuna or corned beef and add to mixture. Mix properly. Pour 4 - 6 cups into steam bag and place in steam pot with boiling water. Steam cook for 2 hours.

Suggested Serving: Let cool and solidify, slice and serve with Jollof rice or fried plantains

INGREDIENTS

FINAL DISH

MUKIMO

(Moh-Kee-Moh) - Serves 4

2 lbs. or 2 large potatoes
1 cup corn and 1 cup beans or 1 can of githeri
1 lb. baby spinach
1 Maggi, Knorr, or ½ a Bouillon cube
½ teaspoon salt or to taste
¼ cup onions
¼ cup green onions
¼ cup vegetable oil
1 cup water

Blend the onions using ½ cup of water. Heat the oil, add the blended onions, and stir. Add salt and Maggi or Knorr cube and continue to stir. Peel and cube potatoes, add to the onion, and let them cook for 3 to 5 minutes. Then add 1 cup of water and bring to a boil. Add the spinach, then the corn and beans (githeri) to the mixture. Cover and let cook. When the spinach is well-cooked and the potatoes are soft, drain any excess stock and set aside. With a potato masher, mash the mixture together, gradually adding the reserved stock a tablespoon at a time to moisten the mixture. It should be firm, like stiff mashed potatoes, not runny and not hard. Adjust seasoning to taste. It is better to turn the heat to low or off and mash while the pot is still hot; this helps to dry up any excess water that is in the mixture and allows the right consistency to be reached.

Note: If dried corn and beans are used, soak overnight, rinse, and cook with salt until well done before making mukimo.

Suggested Serving: Serve by itself or with some chicken or beef stew.

INGREDIENTS

FINAL DISH

TOOH-KOONI

(Mashed Beans & Potatoes)

3 lbs. or 3 large potatoes peeled and cubed
2 cups dried beans or 3 cans of beans
1 cup chopped onion
1 cup palm oil
½ teaspoon ground country onion or
1 teaspoon MammyDoro Beans Seasoning
½ teaspoon MammyDoro African Basil (masepo)
Salt, Maggi, Bouillon or Knorr cubes to taste

If dried beans are used, soak overnight for faster cooking. Rinse and add 5 cups water. Add 1 teaspoon of salt and cook for about 30 minutes or until beans are well done and soft. Strain and set aside. If canned beans are used, rinse properly and set aside. Peel and cube potatoes. Put ½ cup palm oil in a pot and heat for 1 minute; do not bleach. Add onions, salt, Maggi or Knorr or Bouillon cubes. Add potatoes and mix properly. Pour in strained beans and add 2 teaspoons MammyDoro Beans Seasoning and 1 teaspoon MammyDoro African Basil (Nchanwu-masepo). If you do not have these seasonings but have ground "country onion," add ½ teaspoon. Add 1 cup of water, cover the pot, and let the potatoes cook for about 20 minutes over medium heat. Watch to make sure water does not dry up before they are cooked. If water dries up, add ½ cup of water and continue to cook until potatoes are well done, beans are soft, and water dries up.

With a potato masher, begin to mix and mash the potatoes and beans. Turn off the heat and continue to mix and mash until potatoes and beans are properly mashed together. The consistency should be thicker than mashed potatoes but not hard.

Suggested Serving: Serve by itself or with some chicken or beef.

INGREDIENTS

FINAL DISH

RICE

Most people in West Africa live on rice as a staple food. Other foods like cassava, yams, and plantains are only a secondary food item, and a typical Sierra Leonean or Liberian would say, "I have not yet eaten" if all they had was some cassava fufu and light soup, without the most precious bowl of rice. It is only after they have eaten rice with some cassava leaf sauce, potato greens, or stewed crabmeat that they admit they have eaten. Rice is therefore an important part of the diet in the West of Africa, and the diet begins to include other food items like fufu as the geography changes towards Central, East, and South of Africa.

In 1979, in an attempt to encourage domestic rice production, Liberian Minister of Agriculture Florence Chenoweth proposed to raise the price of imported rice from $22 to $26 per 100-pound bag. The prospect of an increase to the cost of their dietary staple outraged Liberians, who, in protest, on April 14, 1979 flooded the streets of Monrovia, Liberia's capital city. More than 12,000 citizens protested, and the ensuing "1979 Rice Riots" have been widely blamed for sparking Liberia's descent into civil war. These riots ushered in a series of assassinations and coups that continued for ten years, until full-blown war broke out in 1989. Many Liberians grow their own rice, sugar cane, and cassava (yucca root). Rice is eaten at least twice a day (more than any other starch). Foreign rice, or pasava, is considered much better than locally grown rice because of the poor harvesting and hauling methods. Palm oil or palm butter is usually served with rice. Cassava leaves and potato leaves are both stewed and eaten with the rice, just like spinach. 85 percent of calories consumed in Liberia come from rice, but after decades of turmoil and war the country relies on imported rice to feed itself—at a very steep cost.

Brown rice is rich in fiber, selenium, and a wide array of antioxidants. The process of removing the hull is the least damaging to the nutritional value of brown rice. When rice is further processed, by polishing to produce white rice, the layer filled with health supportive essential fats is destroyed. The resulting white rice is bereft of its original nutrients. On the other hand, brown rice is found in its near natural state (no perfume added). Though flavor is sacrificed, the brown rice still offers a nutrition benefit. Unfortunately, most of the rice eaten in Africa is polished.

Njanga rice (Crayfish rice) and coconut rice are specific to Cameroon. Njanga rice originated from poor families who were unable to afford all the ingredients for Jollof rice. Today, Njanga rice has satisfied the taste buds of fish lovers and it is no longer considered a dish for the poor. Families actually plan to make this dish for dinner as an alternative to the Jollof rice not because they cannot afford the ingredients for Jollof rice but because of the rich, smoked-fish flavor. It is easier to make than Jollof rice.

Coconut rice is a variant of Jollof rice. Instead of adding several cups of water to the ingredients before adding the rice, one or two cups of water are substituted with coconut milk depending on the quantity of rice that is being cooked. It is therefore called coconut rice. The recipe is the same as jollof rice. Coconut rice is common in West Africa, but it originated from Cameroon. It is a popular dish in most events like weddings, christenings, graduation parties, and any joyous celebrations.

Thiebou jen is the national dish of Senegal. It is a spicy broken rice dish that is seasoned with herbs and spices simmered with vegetables in tomato paste, tamarind, habanero pepper, and stuffed fish. It is very delicious and nutritious, given that it is a mix of carbs, vegetables, and protein.

Pilau is a popular dish in the coast province of Kenya, particularly in the city of Mombasa. It is commonly cooked by the Swahili people, who are the offspring of the intermarriage between Bantus and Arabs. This method of cooking rice has spread to the interior parts of Kenya as a result of intermarriages and trade, even though the Swahili remain the best cooks of this dish to date. Pilau is commonly served in ceremonies, such as weddings, parties, national holidays, and in both Christian and Muslim religious festivals. Pilau is significant in that it acts as a symbol of togetherness and unity of the family. The method of eating Pilau is similar to how Senegalese eat Thiebudienne, by putting Pilau in a large plate or tray and the whole family feeds from it. This is a symbol of the family's togetherness.

BROWN RICE

Serves 3

1 cup brown rice
1 tablespoon coconut oil or olive oil
MammyDoro Pilaf Seasoning
Salt to taste

Wash rice with warm water until running water is clear. Soak for about 10 minutes. Bring 4 cups water to a boil. Add 1 teaspoon of coconut oil or olive oil and ½ teaspoon MammyDoro Pilaf (Jollof) Seasoning and mix. Add rice and cook for 30 minutes on medium heat. Add ½ cup of hot water if rice is not completely cooked. Cover the pot to cook until well done.

Suggested Serving: Serve with any stew or sauce of choice.

INGREDIENTS

FINAL DISH

COCONUT RICE

Vegetarian (Brown rice) - Serves 10

5 cups brown rice
1 cup vegetable oil
1 lb. mixed peas, carrots, and corn
1 red bell pepper (optional)
1 cup chopped onion
1 cup chopped mixed parsley, cilantro, and basil
1 can of tomato paste (6 oz.)
1 can of coconut milk (13.5 oz.)
½ cup chopped garlic
¼ cup chopped ginger
2 teaspoons of MammyDoro Pilaf (Jellof) Seasoning
Salt, Maggi, Knorr, or Bouillon cubes to taste

Soak rice in water for about 30 minutes. It absorbs water and begins to change to white. Blend onions, ginger, garlic, parsley, cilantro, basil, and red bell peppers (if desired) using 1 cup of water. In a large non-stick saucepan, heat oil for 1 minute and pour in blended herbs. Add tomato paste and mix thoroughly. Add Maggi, Knorr, or Bouillon cubes and salt to taste. Continue to stir for 5 minutes and add 4 cups water. Cook for about 45 minutes on medium heat or until water dries off.

In another pot, bring water to a boil and add 1 teaspoon salt. Strain and add the rice into the water. Stir for 15 minutes and strain. In another smaller pot, bring water to a boil, add a pinch of salt, and pour in mixed vegetables. Stir for 5 minutes, strain, and set aside. Open and pour coconut milk into the sauce. Add 4 cups water and bring to a boil. Add 2 teaspoons MammyDoro Pilaf (Jellof) Seasoning, 1 teaspoon curry powder, and pre-steamed rice. Mix, cover firmly, reduce heat and let cook for 25 minutes.

Open and add parboiled vegetables, adjust seasonings to taste and turn off heat. Leave pot covered for 10 minutes on the stove before serving. When rice is properly cooked, mix rice and vegetables to give an even distribution.

Note: You may substitute brown rice with other types of rice. Use the Jollof rice recipe if you do, and replace 1 cup of water with coconut milk. When done, brown rice does not fluff because it still has its bran and germ, which contain oils, as opposed to white rice. Brown rice has a nutty, chewy texture when done.

Suggested Serving: Serve as the entrée for your dinner.

INGREDIENTS

FINAL DISH

A BOOK OF RECIPES, NUTRITIONAL INFORMATION & EDUCATION

JAHICA RICE

(Red Beans & Rice - Wache) - Serves 8   #themotherlandcookbook

3 cups small red beans (preferably dry)
1 cup vegetable oil (preferably olive oil)
½ cup ground crayfish (optional)
2 cups chopped onions
3 chopped roma (plum) tomatoes
1½ cups rice (preferably jasmine)
1 cup chopped spring onions
1 cup chopped leeks
1 can of coconut milk (15 oz.)
1 cup mixed chopped basil, parsley, thyme, cilantro
2 teaspoons of MammyDoro Beans Seasoning
Salt, Maggi, Bouillon, or Knorr cubes to taste

Soak beans overnight with cold water and 1 teaspoon of salt for faster cooking. Pour water out the next day and rinse the beans. Add enough water and salt to taste. Cook beans until done but not soft. Strain and reserve stock in a bowl—will be used later.

If canned beans are used, rinse thoroughly; do not use the stock; contains too much salt.

Blend tomatoes, onions, spring onions, basil, parsley, thyme, and cilantro.

In a larger, non-stick pot:
Heat oil for 1 minute and add crayfish (optional). Add blended herbs into oil and stir for about 10 minutes. Add salt and Maggi, Bouillon, or Knorr cubes to taste. Add finely chopped tomatoes and onions into mixture and cook for about 45 minutes. Add MammyDoro Beans Seasoning and stir. Add coconut milk and stir. Strain 1 cup of bean stock, making sure the muddy part is not added. Add 2 cups water to the mixture and bring to a boil. Add the strained pre-cooked beans into mixture and let boil, mix, and taste for salt. Add rice into the mixture, lower the heat, and cover the pot firmly. Reduce heat to very low—rice is cooked by steam, not flame. After 10 minutes, open and use a wooden spoon to lift up rice and let water descend underneath. Add hot water if needed to cook rice completely. When rice is cooked, mix with the beans to give an even look.

Suggested Serving: Serve with any stew of choice, fried ripe plantains.

INGREDIENTS

FINAL DISH

JOLLOF RICE

(Vegetarian) - Serves 10

5 cups jasmine rice
1 cup olive or coconut oil
1 red bell pepper (optional)
1 can of tomato paste (6oz)
4 Maggi, Knorr or 2 Bouillon cubes to taste
2 teaspoons sea salt or kosher salt to taste
2 teaspoons MammyDoro Pilaf (Jollof) Seasoning
1 cup chopped mixed parsley, cilantro, and basil
6 cloves garlic
½ cup chopped ginger
1 cup chopped onion
½ cup green onions or leeks
7 cups water

Blend onions, leeks, ginger, garlic, parsley, cilantro, basil, and red bell peppers (if desired) using 1 cup of water. In a large non-stick pot, heat oil for 1 minute and add blended herbs into oil. Add tomato paste and mix thoroughly. Add Maggi, Knorr, or Bouillon cubes and salt to taste. Cook for about 45 minutes or until water dries off. Add 7½ cups water and bring to a boil. Add 2 teaspoons of MammyDoro Pilaf (Jollof) Seasoning. Cook for 5 more minutes and add rice, mix, and cover firmly. Let boil for 10 minutes, mix, and reduce heat to very low—rice is cooked by steam, not flame. After 10 minutes, open and use a wooden spoon to lift up rice around the sides of the pot and let water descend underneath. Adjust seasoning to taste and add a little hot water if needed to completely cook rice.

Note: You can add beef or chicken to this dish if you desire. Cut the beef or chicken into bite sizes. Season well, and cook until well done. Fry and add to the rice while cooking. The reason you should fry it is to prevent the meat from getting soft or soggy. If you use basmati, parboiled, or Uncle Ben's rice, estimate water in a ratio of 2:1, water to rice.

Suggested Serving: Serve with stew of choice or baked chicken, grilled fish or stewed vegetables.

INGREDIENTS

FINAL DISH

NJANGA RICE

(Crayfish Rice) - Serves 6

4 cups rice (preferably Jasmine or Basmati)
1 cup crayfish
1 large onion
1 cup chopped leeks
3 cloves of garlic (optional)
2 roma (plum) tomatoes
2 cups palm oil
6 cups water
1 teaspoon MammyDoro African Blue Basil
Salt, Maggi, Bouillon, or Knorr cubes to taste

Blend onions, leeks, and garlic (if used) into paste using 1 cup of water and set aside. Slice tomatoes and squeeze seeds. Put in blender and grind using ½ cup of water and set aside. Grind crayfish using a rolling board and pin or pound in mortar (keep it coarse).

Put palm oil into pot and heat until almost clear (bleaching). Or use vegetable oil of choice if palm oil is unavailable or undesirable. Add crayfish (njanga) into hot oil and stir properly. Add salt and Maggi, Bouillon or Knorr and the blended mixture into the crayfish and stir for 5 minutes. Pour in blended tomatoes and add a teaspoon of African Blue Basil. Let cook for 30 minutes on medium to high heat, stirring occasionally to prevent sauce from sticking and burning, then add 6 cups water and bring to a boil. You can substitute the water with chicken or beef broth for added flavor. Add rice to mixture and stir. Adjust seasonings to taste. Cover pot firmly; reduce heat to low and let cook for 30 minutes (after the first 15 minutes, open and use a wooden spoon to lift up rice around the sides of the pot and let water descend underneath). If more water is needed to completely cook the rice, add hot water as needed. When rice is done, remove from the stove and open the pot.

Suggested Serving: Serve as entrée.

INGREDIENTS

FINAL DISH

PILAU RICE

Serves 8

1 lb. basmati rice
3 lbs. chicken
1 medium onion, chopped
½ cup chopped ginger
½ cup chopped garlic
2 roma (plum) tomatoes, chopped
2 bay leaves
½ teaspoon freshly ground black pepper
1 cup vegetable oil
1 teaspoon ground cinnamon
½ teaspoon coriander
1 habanero pepper (optional)
1 teaspoon Pilau Masala or MammyDoro Pilaf (Jollof) Seasoning
8 cups water
Salt, Maggi, Bouillon, or Knorr cubes to taste

Remove the skin from the chicken, cut into bite sizes. Add 1 teaspoon of salt, black pepper, and 4 Maggi/Bouillon/Knorr cubes to chicken. Mix properly and put aside. Blend pepper, ginger, garlic, and set aside. Heat vegetable oil for about 2 minutes. Add chicken and stir for 10 minutes. Add chopped tomatoes and onions and mix properly. Continue to stir for about 10 minutes. Wash the rice until water runs clear and leave it to soak in cold water for 10 minutes. Add 8 cups water to the chicken and bring it to a boil. Cook for 5 minutes and then add the Pilau spice and coriander and continue to cook for another 10 minutes. Add the rice and mix. Cover and cook on a high heat until water starts to boil; reduce the heat to low and cook until all the water dries off and rice is completely cooked. Check and adjust salt and/or Maggi, Knorr or Bouillon cubes. Add a little hot water if rice is not completely cooked and let simmer until water dries off.

Suggested Serving: Serve as entree.

INGREDIENTS

FINAL DISH

STUFFED TURNIP LEAVES

(A variation of Libyan Lebrak) - Serves 6   #themotherlandcookbook

2 cups rice
1 8 oz. can tomato sauce
1 bunch turnip leaves
1 habanero pepper (optional)
2 teaspoons MammyDoro Meat Seasoning
2 cups chopped vegetables of choice
1 cup chopped parsley, basil, and cilantro
1 teaspoon MammyDoro Pilaf (Jollof) Seasoning
Salt, Maggi, Bouillon, or Knorr cubes to taste
1½ lbs. minced meat
4 scallions
2 teaspoons turmeric
Pinch of cinnamon
1 cup virgin olive oil
½ cup garlic cloves
½ cup ginger

Blend garlic, parsley, basil, cilantro, pepper and scallions and set aside. Cut the stem off the turnip leaves, rinse and set aside. Bring water to a boil. Add ½ teaspoon of salt. Add rice and stir for 5 minutes, strain and put into a large bowl and set aside. Put the meat into a saucepan, add 1 teaspoon of salt, 1 Maggi, Bouillon or Knorr cube. Add blended herbs, and all other seasonings. Mix properly and put saucepan on the stove. Stir for 5 minutes and add chopped mixed vegetables. Continue to stir for another 5 minutes and pour mixture into the pre-cooked rice. Add tomato sauce and mix properly. Taste and adjust seasonings. Put two tablespoons on each turnip green leaf, roll over and fold the edges in an envelope-shape and place it on a piece of foil paper. This helps to keep the contents together without wasting the oil and juice. Pour water in a steaming pot and put on the stove. Place the wrapped leaves into the pot and cook for 45 minutes or until the rice is cooked. Remove gently and sprinkle some olive oil over it and serve.

Note: The original Libyan recipe uses vine leaves. Because these are not readily available, I have used turnip leaves. Also, this variation gives an opportunity to add greens and other vegetables to the dish. I have added butter squash and bell peppers.

Suggested Serving: Serve as a side.

INGREDIENTS

FINAL DISH

THIEBOU DJEN

(Mashed Beans & Potatoes)

6 cups broken rice, jasmine or basmati rice

2 large onions, chopped

4 garlic cloves

1 cup mixed garlic, thyme, parsley

1 can of tomato paste (12 oz.)

5 lbs blue fish, grouper or white-flesh fish

Salt, Maggi, Bouillon or Knorr cubes to taste

1 teaspoon freshly ground black pepper

1lb large green cabbage

MammyDoro Seafood Seasoning

1 cup peanut oil

Escargot (optional)

1 green bell pepper

1 tablespoon tamarind paste

2 large carrots

2 bay leaves

1lb yucca (cassava)

2 limes

1 habanero pepper (optional)

Wash whole fish with lemon or lime juice, cut into steaks about 1½ inches thick, and steep in salted water for about 30 minutes. Cut cabbage into 4 wedges. Peel and cut carrots into thirds. Blend 1 onion, thyme, peppers, and Maggi cubes and put aside. Cube bell peppers and set aside. Dilute tamarind paste in ¼ cup water and set aside. Add salt,   2 teaspoons MammyDoro Seafood Seasoning and rub in properly. Blend parsley, garlic, Maggi, Bouillon, or Knorr cubes and habanero pepper and add to fish. Mix properly.

In a non-stick pot, heat the oil over medium-high. Add chopped onions and stir for 3 minutes. Add thyme, peppers, escargot (optional), and tomato paste and stir for about 15-20 minutes. Put the cabbage, carrots, and yucca into the pot. Carefully place the marinated fish steaks into the sauce. Add 3 cups water and bring to a boil, then lower to a simmer. Cook for about 30 minutes over medium to high heat with pot uncovered, remove the fish when done and let the vegetables continue cooking until they are well done. Remove the vegetables and put into a separate bowl. Wash the rice well under cold running water until the water runs clear. (This will eliminate the extra starch and will make the rice less sticky). Add 3 cups water and add the diluted tamarind paste to the broth. Adjust the seasonings to taste and let simmer for 20 more minutes or until oil rises to the surface of the broth. Remove a few ladles of broth into a separate bowl, add the fish sauce, and stir. Taste the sauce and adjust seasoning again if need be. Add the rice into the pot, returning some of the reserved broth to the pot if necessary, to just cover the rice. Bring to a boil and reduce heat to low. Cover the pot with a tight lid and cook until rice is well done.

Suggested Serving: Serve rice on a platter; distribute vegetables and fish around the platter; cut limes into wedges and garnish platter.

INGREDIENTS

FINAL DISH

THIEBOU KETIAKH

(Hoppin John- Black-eyed peas & Rice)

#themotherlandcookbook

2 cups black-eyed peas
1 cup rice
1 cup olive oil
2 roma (plum) tomatoes
½ cup chopped onions
½ cup chopped leeks or green onions
1 teaspoon MammyDoro Beans Seasoning
½ cup mix parsley, basil, cilantro
½ cup chopped mixed garlic and ginger
Salt, Maggi, Bouillon, or Knorr cubes to taste

Soak beans for 2 hours. Rinse and put into a saucepan. Add 1 teaspoon of salt, 1 teaspoon of MammyDoro Beans Seasoning, and 1 Maggi or Knorr cube. Add 2½ cups water and cook for 20 minutes. Take the pot from the stove to stop beans from continuing to cook. Pour in a bowl and set aside. Add ½ cup of olive oil to the saucepan and heat for a minute or less. Add chopped onions and stir. Then add bended herbs and continue to stir for 5 minutes. Add chopped tomatoes and continue to stir for another 5 minutes. Add 5 cups water and let it cook for 20 minutes. Wash rice until water runs clear. Add to the boiling sauce and mix properly. Pour in the pre-cooked black-eye peas and reduce the heat to medium. Cook for 20 minutes and check to make sure rice is well done. If not, add ½ cup of boiling water and let cook until rice is well done. Mix the rice and the beans and take the pot off the store. Serve as desired.

Suggested Serving: Serve with greens, corn bread and any meat of choice.

INGREDIENTS

FINAL DISH

SOUPS

Soups included here are those that are generally prepared and consumed as an appetizer. They are full of flavor and nutrients. They are also typically consumed in the evenings or after strenuous physical activity.

Achu soup is typically made in Cameroon, and it contains akanwa (limestone) or nihkiy, which is believed to neutralize alcohol in one's system and also contains potassium, calcium and other minerals. This is a very popular soup in Cameroon and is in high demand in the Cameroonian communities in the United States, Europe, and other parts of the world where Cameroonians have settled.

Peppersoup is a generic term for this type of soup even though pepper is just one of the ingredients. It could be made without adding pepper and still be referred to as peppersoup. In Ghana and Liberia, the same consistency of soup is called light soup, which is a more adequate description of the dish given that the stock is only thickened a little bit as opposed to regular stews. The pepper only adds the needed kick to the soup for those who need it, while it can be completely eliminated without losing the flavor of the dish. Peppersoup is commonly sold in restaurants and drinking spots in Cameroon, and sells fast on Saturdays after customers finish their morning sports, be it jogging, tennis, or aerobics.

Watercress is a semi-aquatic perennial herb belonging to the family of Brassicaceae, which is known for both its flavoring and therapeutic and aphrodisiac properties due to its high zinc and iron content. As a good source of vitamin C, chewing watercress also makes teeth stronger. Additionally, vitamin C cures bleeding of the gums or gingivitis. It is believed that the high iodine content in watercress can help prevent goiter, improve the function of the thyroid gland, and relieve symptoms of many forms of hypothyroidism. Watercress usually grows along the banks of slow-running streams and rivers in America, Europe, and Asia and is characterized by its small, round leaves, with a pungent, peppery flavor. On its own, watercress juice is very strong and bitter. To reduce the bitterness, bring water to a boil before putting in the watercress.

Okra soup is very common in West African cuisine. It is mostly used as an accompaniment to any type of fufu. In Nigeria and Cameroon, okra soup is eaten with garri (eba), corn or yam fufu, or water fufu (specifically known as fufu by the Yoruba tribe). In Ghana, it is not uncommon to be served rice and okra soup or okra stew. There is a slight difference in the consistency of the two types of okra dishes.

PUMPKIN

A forgotten superfood, the Pumpkin is a powerhouse of nutrients such as a highly valued omega 3 fatty acids, unsaturated fatty acids, high protein, beta-carotene, vitamin E and minerals like phosphorous, calcium and magnesium. The pumpkin has powerful antioxidants, antidiabetic and anticancer properties. Joshua Arimi PhD. This fruit is never considered on the menu of most families and those who include it do so because of the lack of potatoes, cassava or yams not because of the knowledge of how nutritive it is. A pumpkin is really a squash. It is a member of the Cucurbita family which includes squash and cucumbers. Of the numerous types of pumpkins in the world, only three are common to Africa, the acorn, buttercup and butternut squash. The plant is very important in Southern Nigeria, North West Cameroon, Sierra Leone and Ghana. The leaves are also used in parts of Kenya in making Mukimo as an alternative to spinach. The leaves, the seeds and the flesh are all sources of food and important minerals in African cuisine. In America pumpkins are used to make pies, an important side during Thanksgiving celebrations, dumplings and soups. You can just boil and serve the flesh as an alternative to potatoes, yams or cassava.

PUMPKIN STEW

½ cup chopped ginger & garlic
1 cup chopped onion & leeks
½ cup olive oil
1 lb pumpkin flesh
2 lbs meat or chicken

1 cup chopped parsley, cilantro & basil
½ teaspoon ground nutmeg
Salt, Maggi or Bouillon cube to taste
MammyDoro Meat or Chicken seasoning

Wash and cut meat or chicken into bite sizes. Blend ginger, garlic, parsley, cilantro, basil, leeks and onions and set aside. Cut up a pumpkin into manageable pieces. Remove fiber and seeds. Place in a steamer and cook for 30 minutes or until soft. Let cool, scoop out flesh and place into a blender. Add olive oil into a saucepan and heat for 1 minute. Add beef or chicken, 2 teaspoons of MammyDoro seasoning, Maggi or Bouillon and salt to taste. Stir for 10 minutes and add blended herbs. Continue to stir until chicken or beef is tender. Add a cup or two of water; just enough to cook the meat. Add the pureed pumpkin and bring to the boil. Cover and simmer over a medium heat for 20 minutes, stirring occasionally to prevent stew from sticking and burning. Add nutmeg and freshly ground black pepper. Add a little water to desired thickness if the sauce is too thick. Taste and adjust seasonings as needed.

Suggested serving: Pour over boiled pasta or steamed rice.

ACHU SOUP

Serves 10

3 lbs. cow feet and/or kanda
1 lb. beef (preferably smoked)
2 roma (plum) tomatoes
Kanwa to taste
2 lbs. smoked turkey (optional)
2 cups palm oil (preferably Ola Ola brand)
Salt, Maggi, Knorr, or Bouillon cubes to taste
MammyDoro Achu-Ishewu Seasoning to taste
6 oz. smoked fish
2 lbs. beef tripe
1 red bell pepper
Fresh pepper to taste

Shred and soak smoked fish in cold water. Dissolve akanwa (potash) in a cup of water and set aside. Nihkiy is preferable. Put cut cow feet or kanda in a pot. Add only salt, Maggi, and a cup of diluted akanwa or nihkiy and cook for about 60 minutes. You may cook using a pressure cooker for faster results. If pressure cooker is used, let the pot hiss for 20 minutes, cool, open, and add beef tripe and/or intestines (if desired), one red bell pepper and 2 roma tomatoes and continue to cook for another 20 minutes. Add beef, smoked turkey, and soaked smoked fish and continue to cook for another 20 minutes or until all meats are well done. Separate all meats from stock, including fresh pepper, and let the stock cool down. Add MammyDoro Achu-Ishiewu Seasoning in meat stock, 1 teaspoon at a time, and taste at each addition for concentration. Add pre-heated akanwa solution or nihkiy into the stock 1 tablespoon at a time. Add 1 cup of pre-warmed palm oil into the meat stock (if ola ola is used, do not pre-heat). Using a small bowl, continuously scoop and pour mixture back into pot, lifting your hand up about a foot from the pot. Then pour mixture half-way full into the blender, together with tomatoes and bell pepper. Whip until all the soup is properly mixed, producing a fine, mustard-yellow color. Pour soup into bowl containing pre-cooked meats and continue until all stock is whipped. Put whole boiled peppers into the soup. Taste and adjust seasonings as needed.

Suggested Serving: Serve with achu fufu or as an appetizer.

INGREDIENTS

FINAL DISH

FISH PEPPERSOUP

Serves 4

1 lb. fish fillet (or whole fish) of choice
1 green bell pepper
1 onion
2 garlic cloves
1 medium tomato
6 potatoes or veggie of choice
1 celery stock
1 habanero pepper (or more, if needed; optional)
2 teaspoons MammyDoro Peppersoup Seasoning
Sea salt or kosher salt
Maggi, Bouillon, or Knorr cubes to taste

Wash fish properly with lemon or lime juice (if whole fish is used). Cut fish into desired sizes and add 1 flat teaspoon salt. Add 1 teaspoon MammyDoro Peppersoup Seasoning to fish. Grind a few grains of Njangsa (akpi) and add to fish. Rub in seasonings and salt into fish and put aside. Peel and boil potatoes in another pot.

In a soup pot:
Add 10 cups water and 1 teaspoon MammyDoro Peppersoup Seasoning. Open bell pepper in half, remove seeds, rinse, chop, and add to pot. Peel and chop onion, then add to pot. Chop celery and add to pot. Split tomatoes, squeeze seeds, and add to pot. Add habanero pepper (if used). Add garlic cloves to pot. Add salt and Maggi, Knorr, or Bouillon cubes to taste. Pre-cook all these vegetables until well done (about 45 minutes). Remove vegetables from stock and put into blender. Let cool. Blend and pour into soup pot and bring to a boil. Add water to desired thickness and then add fish. Reduce heat to medium and cook until fish is done (about 15 minutes).

Suggested Serving: Serve hot with boiled potatoes, steamed rice or just as is.

INGREDIENTS

FINAL DISH

GOAT OR COW FEET PEPPERSOUP

Serves 4   #themotherlandcookbook

3 lbs. goat meat or cow feet
1 green bell pepper
1 medium onion
1 celery stalk
½ leeks (bottom white part only)
2 roma (plum) tomatoes
1 habanero pepper (or more, if needed)
2 teaspoons of MammyDoro All-Purpose Seasoning
10 grains of MammyDoro Njangsa spice (optional)
Salt, Maggi, Bouillon, or Knorr cubes to taste

Wash meat of choice, cut into desired sizes, and put in a soup pot with enough water to cover the meat about 2 inches above meat level. Add salt and bring to a boil for about 10 minutes. Strain the meat out of this stock. Skip this step if you use cow feet for your soup. Just wash the cow feet and continue. Put meat of choice into soup pot. Add 2 tablespoons of MammyDoro All-Purpose Seasoning, 2 Maggi or Knorr cubes, and 1 teaspoon of salt. Open green bell pepper, remove seeds, rinse, cut in half, and put into pot. Peel and split onion into two halves and add to pot. Break celery into thirds and add to pot. Cut leeks into thirds and add to pot. Add whole habanero peppers (if desired). Cut tomatoes in half, squeeze out seeds, and add to pot. Cook meat together with vegetables until vegetables are well done. Blend njangsa seeds and sieve into soup pot.
Remove vegetables and put into a blender. Let cool. Add water as needed and blend into fine paste. Blend the habanero pepper as well, if heat is desired. Pour pureed vegetables back into soup pot. Verify and adjust seasonings to taste. Add water to desired thickness and continue to cook until meat is tender.

Suggested Serving: Serve with steamed rice or boiled plantains, yams and potatoes.

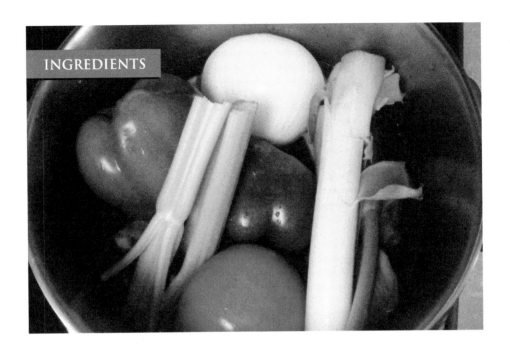

INGREDIENTS

FINAL DISH

KREN KREN SOUP

(Palaver sauce, Molohkia sauce with fish) - Serves 8   #themotherlandcookbook

1 lb. fish (smoked or fresh)
½ cup ground crayfish
1 crab (optional)
½ cup chopped garlic
½ cup chopped ginger
2 habanero peppers (optional)
1 lb. chopped jute leaves (molohkia)
1 cup chopped mixed basil, parsley & cilantro
2 teaspoons MammyDoro All-Purpose Seasoning
6 oz. stock fish or stock fish bits (optional)
Salt, Maggi, Bouillon, or Knorr cubes to taste
½ cup palm oil
1 lb. shrimps (optional)
1 lb. fresh okra (optional)
1 cup chopped onion
1 cup chopped leeks

Soak stock fish overnight to remove pungent smell and facilitate cooking process. If stock fish bits are used, soak for about 2 hours before cooking. Blend onions, ginger, garlic, leeks, parsley, basil, and cilantro. In a saucepan, pour ½ cup of palm oil and heat for 3 minutes on medium heat. Add ground crayfish and stir. Add blended herbs and stock fish (if used). Add 1 teaspoon of salt and 2 Maggi or Knorr cubes or 1 Bouillon cube; cook for 45 minutes or until stock fish is well done. Keep adding 1 cup of water as water dries off while cooking. Blend and add okra, habanero pepper, shrimps, and crab (if used) and cook under low heat for about 10 minutes. Add chopped jute leaves and cook for 10 minutes. Taste and adjust seasonings as needed. Turn off heat, let simmer for about 5 minutes, and serve.

Note: Most Africans who cannot find jute leaves in their neighborhood grocery stores or farmers markets improvise this dish by cooking okra soup and adding chopped spinach. The spinach and the okra feel like the sauce made with the jute leaves. This helps to swallow the fufu, since most people do not chew fufu.

Suggested Serving: Serve with fufu of choice.

INGREDIENTS

FINAL DISH

OKRA SOUP

(Mixed Meats) - Serves 8

2 lbs. meat (beef, chicken, lamb, goat, or a combination)
6 oz. stock fish or stock fish bits (optional)
½ cup ground crayfish
5 bony fish or smoked cat fish (optional)
1 cup chopped mixed basil, parsley and cilantro
1 lb. fresh okra
2 cups chopped ugu (okongobong), bitter leaf, or spinach
½ cup chopped garlic
½ cup chopped ginger
1 cup chopped leeks
1 cup chopped onions
2 habanero peppers (optional)
½ cup palm oil
2 teaspoons MammyDoro All-Purpose Seasoning
Sea salt, Maggi, Bouillon, or Knorr cubes to taste

Soak stock fish overnight to remove pungent smell and facilitate cooking. If stock fish bits and bony fish are used, soak for at least 1 hour before cooking. Blend onions, ginger, garlic, leeks, parsley, basil, and cilantro and set aside. Cut and blend okra and set aside. Cut meat into bite sizes, wash, and set aside. Put palm oil into saucepan and heat for about a minute on medium heat. Do not bleach. Add meat to oil, 1 teaspoon of salt, two Maggi or Knorr cubes, 2 teaspoons of MammyDoro All-Purpose Seasoning, and stir for about 5 minutes. Pour in the blended herbs and stir for 5 minutes. If, ugu(okongobong) or bitter leaf are used, add to meat at this time. Rinse stock fish and add to the meat. Add 2 cups water and cook for about 45 minutes. Add ground crayfish and stir properly. Add blended okra and let simmer for about 15 minutes and serve.

Note: If chopped spinach is used instead of ugu or bitter leaf, add at the end about 3 minutes before okra soup is ready to serve.

Suggested Serving: Serve with fufu of choice.

INGREDIENTS

FINAL DISH

OGBWONO SOUP

Serves 15

2 lbs. beef (or meat of choice)
1 lb. hen
6 oz. stock fish or stock fish bits
1 cup ground crayfish
5 pieces bony dry fish or cat fish
1 cup chopped mixed basil, parsley, and cilantro
1 lb. fresh okra
2 cups spinach or bitter leaf
1 cup ground ogbwono (African mango seed)
½ cup chopped garlic
½ cup chopped ginger
1 cup chopped leeks
1 cup chopped onion
1 cup palm oil
2 teaspoons MammyDoro Meat Seasoning
Salt, Maggi, Bouillon, or Knorr cubes to taste

In a bowl: Soak stock fish overnight to remove pungent smell and facilitate cooking process. If stock fish bits are used instead, soak both stock fish bits and bony fish for about an hour before cooking. Blend onions, ginger, garlic, leeks, parsley, and basil to a fine mixture and set aside. Wash bitter leaf or ugu(okongobong) leaf and set aside. If dried leaves are used, soak them overnight, then rinse and squeeze.

Cut and wash hen and add to saucepan. Pour in blended herbs. Add salt and Maggi or Knorr cubes to taste. Add bitter leaf into saucepan and cook for 45 minutes. Rinse stock fish and add to saucepan. Remove bones from bony fish, blend, and pour into saucepan. Then add meat of choice and continue to cook for another 30 minutes.

In a smaller saucepan: Pour 1 cup of palm oil and heat for a minute. Do not bleach. Add crayfish and stir. Pour ogbwono into oil and crayfish. Continue to stir and add warm water 1 cooking spoonful at a time until ogbwono is thick and fluffy. Then pour it into the pre-cooked meats and reduce the heat. Pour blended okra into mixture and cook for 10 minutes.

Note: If spinach is used instead of bitter leaf, add at the end about 5 minutes before ogbwono soup is ready to serve.

Suggested Serving: Serve with eba (garri), pounded yam, rice, corn or oatmeal fufu.

INGREDIENTS

FINAL DISH

WATERCRESS SOUP

Serves 4

2 tablespoons olive oil
½ cup chopped onions
1 cup chopped leeks
2 small or 1 large sweet potato, peeled and chopped
2 bunches of watercress
½ pound chicken breast
1 teaspoon MammyDoro All-Purpose Seasoning
Salt, Maggi, Bouillon, or Knorr cubes to taste

Put water in a pot and bring to a boil. Add ½ teaspoon of baking soda. Chop up watercress and rinse under running water. Add watercress and cook for 5 minutes. Remove and strain. Put in a bowl with cold water to stop the cooking process.
Blend leeks and onions into a coarse puree, not fine like a paste. Cut chicken or meat of choice into small pieces and put into a soup pot. Pour in blended leeks and onions. Add salt, Maggi, Knorr, or Bouillon cubes to taste. Add 1 teaspoon of MammyDoro All-Purpose Seasoning. Cook for about 25 minutes. Add chopped sweet potatoes. Cook for another 10 minutes and add watercress to boiling pot. Add 2 teaspoons of olive oil (optional). Cook for about 5 minutes.

Suggested Serving: Serve hot.

INGREDIENTS

FINAL DISH

SWEET POTATOES

Sweet potato roots are a good source of carbohydrates, while the leaves contain additional nutritional components in much higher concentrations than in many other commercial vegetables. They are cooked as a vegetable in several parts of the world, and it is a delicacy in the countries of Liberia, Sierra Leone, and several Asian countries. The top 4 inches of the tips, including the stem and the new and tender parts of the leaves, are the preferred edible parts of the sweet potato greens. Sweet potatoes are grown in the North West Region of Cameroon, but the leaves are only used as feed for livestock. They are rich in vitamin B, beta-carotene, iron, calcium, zinc, and protein, and the crop is more tolerant of diseases, pests, and high moisture than many other tubers. Their annual yield is much higher than many other green vegetables because the leaves can be harvested several times a year. It is a versatile plant, as it is used as food, as livestock feed, and for starch and alcohol production.

Sweet potatoes also have a low glycemic index. The stew from sweet potato greens is very delicious. In the US, you can find sweet potato leaves in your local farmer's markets. Add this to your list of greens and enjoy the many medicinal and nutritive benefits of both the roots and the greens, a few of which are its anti-inflammatory, antioxidant, and high dietary properties.

STEWS

African stews are typically tomato-based; however, Senegalese onion stew does not require any tomatoes. To maximize the benefits of tomatoes, use methods that require longer cooking times for tomatoes. Since tomatoes are acidic, it is advantageous to cook them longer so that they taste better and decrease acid reflux.

Depending on the type of stew, the tomatoes are processed differently. Because meats take longer to cook and require sauce for the stew, the tomatoes are ground into a puree and added to the meat. With stewed vegetables, the tomatoes are chopped because they cook faster this way.

Stews will look and taste differently depending on the other herbs and spices that are added when cooking. A typical Nigerian stew is bright red in color due to the use of red bell peppers and red hot habanero peppers. On the other hand, if herbs like ginger, garlic, basil, celery, bay leaves, parsley, and cilantro are added to the meat to enhance the flavor, the final color of the stew will be brown or a dark red.

Tomatoes are rich in potassium, a mineral of which most of us don't get enough. They contain all three high-powered antioxidants: beta-carotene, Vitamin A, and Vitamin C. The tomato skin also holds most of the flavonols (another family of phytochemicals that includes quercetin and kaempferol). So, to maximize the health properties of tomatoes, don't peel before cooking. Also, researchers have found that the longer the tomatoes are cooked, the better the rate of absorption of the lycopene.

Palm butter is another thickener that is commonly used in West Africa. This is made from the juice of fresh palm nuts and is called banga soup. This is the natural unprocessed butter from palm nuts. This is commonly used in palm oil producing countries of West Africa, such as the Ivory Coast, Liberia, Burkina Faso, Ghana, and Cameroon.

Peanut butter, which is used as a thickener for stews, provides a healthy alternative to starches and flour that are used in other parts of the world. Peanut butter stew is very popular in Guinea, Gambia, Ghana, Cameroon, Zimbabwe, Zambia, and Senegal.

For people allergic to peanuts but who can tolerate almonds, I have created almond butter stew as an alternative thickener to mimic this dish so they would not be left out. The same recipe for peanut butter stew works fine with almond butter.

BEEF STEW

Serves 6

3 lbs. beef
8 cloves of garlic
½ cup chopped ginger
1 cup chopped onions
1 cup chopped leeks, parsley, and basil
2 large potatoes
4 carrots
1 teaspoon curry powder (optional)
1 canned tomato paste (6 oz.)
1 canned tomato sauce (29 oz.)
1 cup vegetable oil
2 teaspoons MammyDoro Meat Seasoning
Salt, Maggi, Bouillon, or Knorr cubes to taste

Blend ginger, garlic, basil, parsley, onions, basil, and put aside. Peel and slice carrots. Peel, cube, and wash potatoes and put aside. Cut meat into bite sizes and wash. Put meat into pot, add water and salt, and boil for 20 minutes. Strain, add 2 teaspoons of MammyDoro Meat Seasoning, 1 teaspoon of salt, 4 Maggi cubes, mix properly, and put aside. Put 1 cup of oil into a deep saucepan, heat for about 1 minute, add blended herbs into oil, add tomato paste, and stir for about 5 minutes. Add tomato sauce and 6 cups water. Let cook for about 25 minutes; add carrots, potatoes, meat, and curry powder. Mix properly; reduce heat to medium and let cook for 25 minutes.

Suggested Serving: Serve with steamed rice or jollof rice.

CHICKEN STEW

Serves 6

3 lbs. chicken
6 cloves of garlic
½ cup chopped ginger
1 cup chopped onions,
1 cup chopped leeks, parsley, and basil
Sea salt, Maggi, Bouillon, or Knorr cubes to taste
2 large potatoes
4 carrots
1 canned tomato paste (6 oz.)
1 canned tomato sauce (16 oz.)
2 cups vegetable oil
2 teaspoons MammyDoro Chicken Seasoning

Blend ginger, garlic, basil, parsley, onions, basil, and put aside. Slice carrots, peel and cube potatoes, and put aside. Take skin off of chicken, wash, and cut into bite sizes. Put vegetable oil in pot and heat for about 1 minute. Put chicken into pot and stir properly. Add 2 teaspoons of MammyDoro Chicken Seasoning and mix properly. Continue to stir for 15 minutes; remove and put into separate container. Add blended herbs into remaining oil, add tomato paste. Stir for 5 minutes. Add tomato sauce and 6 cups water and let cook for about 35 minutes. Add carrots, potatoes, and chicken. Adjust seasoning to taste and reduce heat to medium and let cook for 25 minutes.

Suggested Serving: Serve with steamed rice, plantains or yams.

CURRY CHICKEN STEW

Serves 6

4 lbs. chicken
3 teaspoons of curry or as desired
1 cup vegetable oil
Sea salt or kosher salt to taste
Maggi, Bouillon, or Knorr cubes to taste
2 teaspoons MammyDoro Chicken Seasoning
10 roma (plum) tomatoes
1 large onion
6 oz. tomato paste
½ cup chopped leeks
½ cup chopped green onions
½ cup chopped ginger
½ cup chopped garlic
1 cup mixed chopped basil, parsley and cilantro

Take skin off and cut chicken into small pieces. Wash properly and place in a saucepan. Add 2 teaspoons MammyDoro Chicken Seasoning, Maggi, Bouillon or Knorr cubes, and salt to taste. Split each tomato, squeeze seeds, rinse, and add to the chicken. Peel and cut onions in 4 portions and add to the chicken. Add a cup of water and cook for about 25 minutes and set aside. Blend leeks or green onions, ginger, garlic, basil, cilantro and parsley. Pour half into the chicken and set the rest aside.
Pour 1 cup vegetable oil into the pot, heat for about 2 minutes, and add the blended herbs into the hot oil. Open tomato paste and add to mixture. Stir for about 30 minutes. Blend pre-cooked tomatoes and onions and add to mixture. Add 3 teaspoons of curry or to taste. Pour pre-cooked chicken into the sauce, stir, and add hot water to desired thickness. Let simmer for 20 minutes, reduce heat to low until ready to serve.

Suggested Serving: Serve with Jollof rice, Steamed rice or Peas and Rice.

INGREDIENTS

FINAL DISH

EGGPLANT STEW

(Sauce Aubergines) - Serves 8

1 lb. meat of choice (lamb, beef, chicken, pork)
1 onion, chopped
2 eggplants cubed
¼ cup chopped ginger
4 cloves of garlic
2 lbs. mushrooms (optional)
1 cup mixed chopped basil, parsley & cilantro
1 habanero pepper (optional)
2 teaspoons MammyDoro All-Purpose Seasoning
10 grains of MammyDoro Njangsa Spice
Salt, Maggi, Bouillon, or Knorr cubes to taste
½ cup of olive oil
1 onion, whole
1 teaspoon curry powder
¼ cup njangsa
4 roma (plum) tomatoes

If meat is used, wash and put in separate pot. Add tomatoes, sliced onions, garlic cloves, sliced ginger (do not blend yet), and MammyDoro All-Purpose Seasoning. Add enough water to cook the meat. Add salt, Maggi/Bouillon/Knorr cubes to taste. Grind njangsa spice using 1 cup of water and sieve over the meat. Cook until vegetables are well done. If meatless, pre-cook above-mentioned vegetables and herbs until well-done. Remove vegetables, blend into a purée, and put aside. Heat vegetable oil in another pot over medium heat. Add the chopped onions, stir. Add the blended basil, parsley, and cilantro. Let cook until onions are translucent. Add cubed eggplant and stir for 10 minutes. Optionally, add chopped mushrooms. Add in all the seasonings, curry, and cook for at least 5 minutes. Stir in the purée pre-made, pre-cooked meat if used, then let simmer for about 15 minutes. Add a little water to the stew to desired consistency, if too thick.

Serving Suggestion: Serve with Steamed rice, pasta or fufu of choice.

INGREDIENTS

FINAL DISH

GOAT OR OXTAIL STEW

Serves 6

2 lbs. goat or oxtail
½ cup vegetable oil
2 teaspoons MammyDoro Meat Seasoning
8 roma (plum) tomatoes
1 large onion
1 cup mixed chopped ginger, onions, garlic
1 cup chopped green onions, basil, parsley, cilantro
Pepper to taste
1 can of tomato paste (6 oz.)
1 can of tomato sauce (29 oz.)
Salt, Maggi, Bouillon, or Knorr cubes to taste

Split tomatoes, squeeze out the seeds, blend, and set aside. Put goat/oxtail in a large pot and add water and salt. Cook for about 10 minutes, strain, and put aside. Blend the ginger, garlic, pepper, green onions, onions, basil, parsley, and cilantro and put aside. Put vegetable oil in saucepan and heat for 3 minutes. Add goat or oxtail, Maggi, Bouillon, or Knorr cubes and mix properly. Add MammyDoro Meat Seasoning and the blended herbs; continue to stir for about 5 minutes over medium to high heat. Open tomato paste and add to meat. Continue to stir for another 5 minutes. Add blended tomatoes to meat. Open and pour in tomato sauce. Add 5 cups water or enough to cook the meat. Cook for about 45 minutes over medium heat or until meat is tender and water dries up, leaving just a smooth stew.

Note: Pre-boil the meat with salt to reduce the gaminess and the excess grease. It is still going to be very tasty because the taste comes from the herbs and not the grease. Be kind to your arteries.

Suggested Serving: Serve with steamed rice and fried plantains or as needed.

INGREDIENTS

FINAL DISH

KAHTI KAHTI CHICKEN

(Palm oil BBQ Chicken stew) - Serves 6   #themotherlandcookbook

1 chicken (preferably whole, free range chicken)
2 cups palm oil
1 large onion
2 roma (plum) tomatoes
2 teaspoons of MammyDoro Chicken Seasoning
1 teaspoon MammyDoro African Blue Basil (masepo/nchanwu)
Salt, Maggi, Knorr, or Bouillon cubes to taste

Cut up chicken into 4 parts, marinate with salt and Maggi, Knorr or Bouillon cubes. Place chicken on the grill (do not remove skin; fat melts during grilling and shields chicken from drying up and burning). After grilling chicken (half-cooked), cut into bite sizes and put in a large saucepan. Blend onion and tomatoes. Add to the chicken, along with 5 cups water or as needed to cook the chicken. Do not add too much water. Add 2 cups palm oil, 1 teaspoon of MammyDoro African Basil, and 2 teaspoons of MammyDoro Chicken Seasoning. Add salt and Maggi to taste and cook until chicken is tender.

Suggested Serving: Serve with greens of choice, corn fufu, oatmeal fufu, or steamed rice.

OFADA STEW

(Green Pepper Stew) - Serves 15

6 Large Green bell peppers (optional) Or
4 green habanero peppers
6 dry Fish (stock fish) optional
¼ cup Iru, dawadawa or ogiri (optional)
2 cups chopped parsley, basil, cilantro
1 cup leeks/green onions
2 teaspoons MammyDoro Meat Seasoning
6 dry smoked fish (bonny, catfish or kini)
5 lbs. assorted meat (beef, cow feet, tripe,
liver, kidneys)
Salt, Maggi Knorr or Bouillon cubes to taste

12 jalapeño peppers
1 cup chopped onions
½ cup Crayfish
½ cup ginger
½ cup garlic
2 roma (plum) tomatoes
2 cups palm oil

Cut all meats in bite sizes, wash, and set aside. Deseed, wash, and blend the peppers and set aside. If you choose to use jalapeño peppers, do not add habanero peppers because jalapeños are hot. This sauce is a very spicy sauce, so habaneros provide the desired heat if green bell peppers are used. Soak the stock fish and dry fish and remove bones from the dry fish when soft. Blend together ginger, garlic, leeks, onions, parsley, cilantro, basil, and set aside. Blend tomatoes separately and set aside. In a large saucepan, add cow feet/cow skin, salt, and Maggi or Knorr or Bouillon cubes to taste. Cook for 45 minutes. Add beef tripe and half the blended herbs and continue to cook for another 30 minutes. Then add stock fish, dry fish, and blended tomatoes and cook for another 30 minutes. You do not need too much stock, so use just enough water to cook the meats until they are well done.

In another saucepan, add 2 cups palm oil and heat it up for 5 minutes. Be careful not to overcook the oil because it will become dark and have a soapy taste in your stew. After bleaching the oil, move pot away from the stove and let it cool for 5 minutes. Pour in ground crayfish and stir. Add the remaining blended herbs. Bring pot back to the stove and turn it on to medium-high heat. Stir continuously for 15 minutes and pour in blended peppers. Continue to stir for 45 minutes or until water dries off. Add all the pre-cooked meats and stock and mix properly. There should not be more than 4 cups stock. Reduce heat to medium, taste, and adjust seasonings (dawada, iru, ogiri). Let simmer for 20 minutes.

Suggested Serving: Serve over steamed rice (traditionally the rice is placed on a leaf, e.g., banana leaf, and the sauce and meat are poured over the rice).

INGREDIENTS

FINAL DISH

ONION STEW

(Yassa) - Serves 8   #themotherlandcookbook

Meat of choice (Senegalese prefer lamb)
2 cups vegetable oil
6 cups chopped onions
1 lime or lemon
2 green bell peppers
2 tablespoons mustard
4 cloves garlic
1 teaspoon freshly ground black pepper
1/3 cup water
2 teaspoons MammyDoro Meat Seasoning

Cut lamb into desired sizes. In a separate pot, add lamb and salt to the water. Bring to a boil for about 25 minutes. Remove from stock, add MammyDoro Meat Seasoning and put aside. Cut and squeeze lime or lemons in a small cup. Peel and chop up onions and bell peppers. Mix up onions and peppers in a large bowl. Add salt, Maggi, Bouillon, or Knorr cubes to taste. Add mustard and lime and mix properly.

In a large skillet, heat oil over medium heat. Add marinated onions and stir in garlic. Cook for about 20 minutes. Add the pre-cooked lamb and stir.
Reduce heat to low, cover, and let simmer for 20 minutes. Add more water if necessary to prevent sticking. Open and stir until water dries off.

Suggested Serving: Serve over steamed rice.

PEANUT OR ALMOND BUTTER STEW

(Groundnut soup) - Serves 8   #themotherlandcookbook

3 lbs. chicken or meat of choice (beef, pork, goat, chicken, turkey)
½ cup chopped garlic
½ cup chopped ginger
2 small onions
3 roma (plum) tomatoes
1 cup chopped leeks
1 cup mixed chopped basil, cilantro, and parsley
2 cups vegetable oil
1 canned tomato paste (12 oz.)

Salt, Maggi, Bouillon, or Knorr cubes to taste
MammyDoro Chicken or Meat Seasoning
Natural creamy peanut or almond butter
If meat other than chicken is used, follow alternate method for first steps.

Put 4 cups water into a small pot. Split tomatoes in half, squeeze seeds, and put into pot. Cut 2 onions in half and add to pot. Cook for 40 minutes and let cool. Blend leeks, parsley, basil, ginger, cilantro, onion, and garlic and set aside. Cut chicken, take skin off, rinse, put aside. Pour 1 cup vegetable oil into saucepan; add chicken, salt, and 2 Maggi or Knorr cubes or 1 Bouillon cube. Add 2 teaspoons of MammyDoro Chicken Seasoning. Stir for 15 minutes on medium to high heat. Remove chicken and put into a bowl.

Common steps: Pour a cup of vegetable oil into saucepan and heat for about 1 minute. Pour blended herbs into the oil. Open tomato paste and add into oil. Stir for about 30 minutes. Blend pre-boiled tomatoes and onions and pour into sauce. Add pre-cooked chicken or meat and continue to cook for 25 minutes. Add 1 teaspoon curry and stock from pre-cooked meat to desired thickness and lower the heat. Add 3 tablespoons of natural creamy peanut or almond butter and stir for about 10 minutes on medium heat. Adjust sauce to desire thickness.

*Alternate method: Cut and wash meat, put in saucepan; add enough water to cover the meat. Add a teaspoon of salt and boil for 10 minutes. Strain and put in clean saucepan. Add 2 teaspoons of MammyDoro Meat Seasonings, Maggi or Knorr cubes, and salt to taste. Add ½ cup of oil, cook for 20 minutes. Continue with common steps above.

Note: To make peanut butter soup, simply add more tomatoes and onions, vegetables of choice (okra, eggplant) and add water to give a soupy texture.

Suggested Serving: Serve with steamed rice, or fufu of choice.

INGREDIENTS

FINAL DISH

A BOOK OF RECIPES, NUTRITIONAL INFORMATION & EDUCATION

PALM BUTTER STEW

(Mbanga Soup) #themotherlandcookbook

1 lb. can of palm butter cream
1 lb. beef (or meat of choice)
6 oz. smoked fish
1 cup crayfish
6 oz. stock fish
½ cup palm oil
½ cup chopped ginger
4 cloves garlic
½ cup chopped leeks
1 cup chopped onions
½ cup chopped basil, parsley, and cilantro
½ lb. chopped spinach or bitter leaf of ugu (okongobong) leaf
2 teaspoons Mammy Doro All-Purpose Seasoning
Salt, Maggi, Bouillon, or Knorr cubes to taste
Fresh pepper (optional)

Soak smoked fish and stock fish for about an hour for faster cooking. Blend ginger, garlic, leeks, onions, basil, parsley, and cilantro and set aside. Grind crayfish and set aside. Cut meat into bite sizes, wash, and put into pot. Pour half of the blended ingredients into the meat. Add Maggi, salt to taste. Add soaked fish and chopped ugu (okongobong) leaves or bitter leaf and cook until well done. Then set aside.
In another pot, put ½ cup of palm oil and heat just enough to melt the oil. Do not bleach. Add crayfish and stir. Add remaining blended herbs and stir for 20 minutes. Add palm butter cream and stir properly. Add stock from precooked meats. Cook for 45 minutes or until oil rises to the top of the sauce. Then pour in the pre-cooked meats and stir. (If using spinach, do not add to meat at this time.) Adjust seasonings as needed. If spinach is used, add to the meat at the end about 5 minutes before taking pot off the stove.

Suggested Serving: Serve with fufu of choice or steamed rice.

INGREDIENTS

FINAL DISH

PUMPKIN SEED STEW

(Egusi Soup with mixed meats) - Serves 8   #themotherlandcookbook

2 cups ground pumpkin seeds (Egusi)
2 lbs. meat of choice (goat, beef, chicken, or mixed)
6 oz. smoked fish (stock fish, bony fish)
2 cups chopped ugu (okongobong), bitter leaf or spinach
1 cup chopped onion
1 cup chopped leeks

½ cup chopped mixed garlic, ginger
1 cup chopped mixed basil, parsley, and cilantro
2 cups palm oil
½ cup ground crayfish
4 Knorr or Maggi cubes, or 2 Bouillon cubes
Salt to taste

If green pumpkin seeds are used, soak overnight for easy washing. Rub the pumpkin seeds to remove green coating as much as possible (the coating tends to have a pungent, bitter taste). Rinse properly and grind a cup at a time using 1 cup of water. If ground pumpkin seeds are used, pour into a bowl, add a little lukewarm water, mix into a paste, and set aside. An hour before making the soup, soak bony fish/stock fish in a bowl with fish completely submerged in water. Blend onions, mixed basil, parsley, cilantro, garlic, ginger, and leeks and set aside.

Wash meat and put into pot with enough water to cook your meat of choice. Add half blended herbs, 2 Knorr or Maggi cubes or 1 Bouillon cube and a teaspoon of salt into meat. If dried ugu (okongobong) or bitter leaf is used, soak overnight to reduce cooking time. Rinse, squeeze, and add to meat. If collard, turnips, or mustard greens are used, put into a blender and grind into a coarse blend. Drain, squeeze, and add to meat. Strain smoked fish, remove bones, and add to meat. Cook meat, fish, and greens until tender, occasionally adding a cup of water as needed. Set aside when done. Add palm oil into a saucepan and heat for 2 minutes or until hot. Do not bleach. Add ground crayfish and stir briskly. Add the rest of the blended herbs, a teaspoon of salt, and 2 Knorr/Maggi cubes. Stir the mixture for about 20 minutes on high to medium heat. Add the ground pumpkin seeds (egusi) into the saucepan and reduce the heat to medium. Stir-fry until pumpkin seed paste begins to thicken. Do this for about 30 minutes or when you notice the oil rises to the top of the paste. Add the meat and stock fish, mix thoroughly, and let cook for about 10 minutes.

If spinach is used instead of the greens above, squeeze and add to the pumpkin seeds sauce and let cook for about 5 minutes. If too thick, add 1 – 2 cups hot water and stir. Adjust seasonings to taste.

Suggested Serving: Serve with rice, fufu of choice (pounded yam, cassava, farina, amala, gari or oatmeal).

TOMATO STEW

(Vegetarian)

4 roma (plum) tomatoes
½ cup chopped garlic
2 cups chopped onions
1 can of tomato paste (12 oz.)
1 can of tomato sauce (29 oz.)
1 cup chopped leeks
1 teaspoon curry (optional)
1 cup mixed basil, parsley, cilantro
Vegetable oil (preferably olive or coconut oil)
Salt, Maggi, Knorr, or Bouillon cube to taste
2 teaspoons MammyDoro Vegetable Seasoning

Blend leeks, parsley, basil, ginger, garlic, and onions using a cup of water and set aside. Pour 1 cup vegetable oil into a saucepan; heat for about 3 minutes on medium. Open canned tomato and add to hot oil, stirring vigorously. This step helps to eliminate the acidity in the tomato paste. Stir for about 5 minutes. Pour blended herbs into the oil, add 1 teaspoon of salt, 2 teaspoons of MammyDoro Vegetable Seasoning, 1 teaspoon of curry, 2 Maggi or Knorr cubes or 1 Bouillon cube, and continue to stir for about 20 minutes on medium heat. Blend and add tomato into the pot. Stir for about 10 minutes.

Add 4 cups water and cook for 45 minutes or until water dries up. Taste and adjust seasonings as needed.

Suggested Serving: Serve with rice, potatoes, plantains or fufu.

INGREDIENTS

FINAL DISH

KALE

Kale is a very good source of vitamins, dietary fiber, calcium, potassium, vitamin E, vitamin B2, iron, magnesium, vitamin B1, omega-3 fatty acids, phosphorus, protein, folate, and niacin. Kale is a very versatile and nutritious vegetable. It is widely recognized as an incredibly nutritious leaf vegetable since ancient times. Other greens, such as spinach, cannot come close in comparison to the number of nutrients that kale provides. If you make ndole and are out of bitter leaf, try blending kale as an alternative. If you do, a very good idea would be to use the juice after blending and squeezing the kale to make a nutritious, delightful kale juice. Simply add a natural sweetener, like oranges or carrots, and enjoy all the benefits that kale provides. Keep juice refrigerated for up to 3 days. If you have made a lot of juice and cannot consume all of it in three days, keep bottles of it in the freezer and take out as needed. This is live food and will get bad quickly. You get two in one: kale sauce and juice.

VEGETABLES

Dark green leafy vegetables, such as mustard greens, lettuce, kale, chicory, spinach, and chard as well as cruciferous vegetables like broccoli, cauliflower, cabbage, brussels sprouts, bok choy, and kale have an abundance of fiber, folate, and carotenoids. These nutrients may help protect against cancer of the mouth, larynx, pancreas, lung, skin, and stomach. Eggplants (Aubergines) have low calories and are rich in soluble fiber. They come in a wide variety of shapes, sizes, and colors. They contain phenolic flavonoid phyto-chemicals and are a good source of valuable minerals. There are the large dark purple eggplants (American), the medium-sized light purple (Asian) and the green round eggplants (Indian and African). The Garden Huckleberry, dark blue in color when ripe, is considered tasteless, with an irritating metallic aftertaste. In the NW Region of Cameroon, the average Cameroonian enjoys a meal of corn fufu, roasted chicken and garden huckleberry leaves ("contri njama njama"). The flavor from the cooked leaves of the garden huckleberry plant is the same as that of watercress. Potato greens are consumed in several African countries (Liberia, Sierra Leone, Guinea, Mali, and the Ivory Coast). Most other African countries grow sweet potatoes and use the leaves as feed for pigs. It is surprising how other African countries ignore this delicious vegetable. On a scale of 1 to 10, sweet potato leaves rank 10 for most nutritive vegetable and is probably the only one at that level. Liberians refer to it as potato greens, because it is the young green leaf that is used to make this very tasty sauce. Ndole is a sauce made from bitter leaf and is one of the national dishes of Cameroon. Ndole is the sauce that a visitor will remember and long for after visiting Cameroon. Bitter leaf has a very bitter taste, as the name suggests, but the processing method reduces the bitterness and the final dish is a very delicious sauce that is appreciated by almost every visitor to Cameroon.

Eru is a forest leaf whose only known nutritional value is dietary fiber. Most visitors to Cameroon and Nigeria remember this dish when they return to their home countries. It is also amazing how kids, whether born in Africa or abroad, enjoy this dish with either pounded yam, gari, or oatmeal fufu. Edika ikong is a variation of the eru dish. The main leaf used in this dish is the fluted pumpkin leaf. Spinach is also added to soften this leaf while cooking, as is a bit of eru as well. The dish is also characterized by the variety of meats that are included when cooking. It is one of the signature dishes of the people of the Cross River in Nigeria. Cassava leaf is the main vegetable of the countries of the Congo basin—Rwanda, Burundi, Congo Brazzaville, Congo Democratic, Central African Republic, Southern Cameroon, Guinea, Gambia, Liberia, and Sierra Leone. It has a wonderful taste and flavor; no wonder Sierra Leoneans do not make any excuse for their passion of rice. The two together make a great combination.

3-GREENS

(Vegetarian) - Serves 8

1 lb. chopped collards
1 lb. chopped kale, mustards, or turnips
1 lb. chopped spinach
1 cup chopped leeks or spring onions
1 cup chopped onions
1 cup chopped mixed basil, parsley, cilantro
1 cup vegetable oil
3 roma (plum) tomatoes
2 tablespoons MammyDoro Vegetable Seasoning
Salt, Maggi, Knorr, or Bouillon cubes to taste

Boil water. Add ½ teaspoon salt, ½ teaspoon baking soda, and greens of choice, leaving out spinach. Let cook for 15 minutes, checking often to make sure greens are not over-cooked (blanching). Put spinach in another large bowl and add cold water (spinach should not be cooked). When greens are cooked to desired softness, take the pot off the stove, strain, and add the greens into the bowl containing cold water and chopped spinach. Mix properly, squeeze, and set aside.

Heat vegetable oil for about 3 minutes on medium-high. Add chopped onions, 1 teaspoon of salt, 2 Maggi or Knorr cubes or 1 Bouillon cubes Stir for 3 minutes, add chopped tomatoes to mixture and continue to stir for another 5 minutes. Add blended leeks or spring onions, parsley, cilantro, and basil to the sauce. Cook for about 30 minutes.

If non-vegetarian version is needed
Add chopped smoked turkey and 2 cups water
Add ½ cup ground crayfish and cook until turkey is well done

Continue, either method
Add 2 tablespoons of MammyDoro Vegetable Seasoning and mix. Add pre-cooked greens, mix, and reduce heat to low. Continue to mix until water dries up.

Suggested Serving: Serve as a side with any dish.

AMARANTH

(Callaloo, Green) - Serves 8

5 bundles of Callaloo (green)
1 habanero pepper (optional)
1 cup ground crayfish
3 lbs fresh fish (tilapia or mackerel)
2 cup mixed parsley, cilantro & basil
2 teaspoons MammyDoro Vegetable Seasoning
1 teaspoon MammyDoro Seafood Seasoning
Salt, Maggi or Knorr or 1 Bouillon cube to taste
2 cups cooking oil
3 cups chopped onion
10 fresh roma (plum) tomatoes
2 cups chopped leeks

Wash the fish with lime or lemon juice, rinse, and cut into 3-inch sizes. Add a teaspoon of MammyDoro Seafood Seasoning and 1 teaspoon of salt and set aside. This step is best done overnight for better tasting fish. Slice the greens very finely and put into a large bowl. Add two teaspoons of salt and rub the greens until the leaves become translucent. Rinse, squeeze, and set aside. Slice the onions, leeks, and tomatoes and set aside. In a large sauce pan, add 2 cups olive oil and heat for 1 minute. Add fish and fry over medium heat. Flip the side when one side is cooked. Remove fish and place in a bowl. Allow it to cool. Remove the bones from the fish and set aside. Using the same oil used in frying the fish, remove any debris from the fish and add onions and leeks. Stir for 5 minutes and add tomatoes. If oil reduced too much when frying the fish, add 1 cup of oil and continue to stir the onions, leeks, and tomatoes for another 10 minutes. Add blended parsley, cilantro, and basil. Add 1 cup of water and let cook for 20 minutes. Add greens and stir. Continue to stir and reduce the heat. Do not cover the pot. Stir the greens until they are done. Then add the fish and mix. Take pot off the stove and serve.

Suggested Serving: Serve with yams, plantains or rice.

INGREDIENTS

FINAL DISH

CASSAVA LEAF SAUCE

Serves 8

3 lbs. frozen cassava leaves (or dried)
½ pound smoked chicken, fish
1 cup chopped leeks
1 habanero pepper (optional)
Salt, Maggi, or Knorr cubes to taste
1 cup mixed chopped garlic and ginger
1 lb. spinach (if dried cassava leaves are used)
1 cup chopped parsley, leeks, cilantro, and basil
2 teaspoons MammyDoro Meat Seasoning
1 lb. meat of choice
1 large onion
1 cup ground crayfish
1 - 2 cups palm oil
Pepper to taste

If dried cassava leaf is used, soak it overnight for ease of cooking. Soak the smoked fish for about 3 hours before cooking, depending on how dry the fish is. If regular stock fish is used, soak overnight to remove pungent smell and reduce cooking time. The spinach should be used as a tenderizer for the cassava leaves. Blend parsley, leeks, cilantro, basil, onion, ginger, and garlic and set aside. In a large saucepan, add meat, salt, Maggi, or Knorr cubes and half of the blended herbs. Add 2 teaspoon MammyDoro Meat Seasoning. Add enough water and cook meat until tender, depending on your choice of meat. Add palm oil into a saucepan and heat for about 2 minutes (do not bleach). Add crayfish and stir. Add the remaining blended herbs, then and add smoked fish and chicken. Cook for 20 minutes. Add spinach and stir properly. Rinse and squeeze cassava leaves and add to pot. Mix properly and let it simmer for 30 minutes, stirring frequently to prevent it from burning. Add some beef stock 1 cup at a time and watch the consistency. Add pre-cooked meats and let simmer for 20 minutes on medium to low heat. If peanut butter is desired, add peanut butter or groundnut paste at this time. Adjust seasonings to taste.

Suggested Serving: Serve with steamed rice.

EDIKA IKONG

Serves 14

3 lbs. goat, beef, or mixed meats
½ lb. dried ukazi leaf
8 oz. stock fish
1 large onion
4 green onions
Salt, Maggi, Bouillon, or Knorr to taste
2 teaspoons MammyDoro Meat Seasoning
2 cups chopped mixed parsley, basil, cilantro
4 lbs. fresh baby spinach or frozen chopped spinach
6 cups dried ugu leaf
2 cups ground crayfish
4 pieces of dried fish
1 cup chopped leeks
2 cups palm oil
Snails, periwinkle (optional)

If mixed meats (tripe, cow-feet, goat meat) are used, cook with salt and Maggi or Knorr cubes to taste and set aside. If snails and periwinkle are used, cook them together with the mixed meats. Soak ugu(okongobong) leaf in water for about 20 minutes. Soak stock fish bits in water and set aside. If dried ukazi(eru) leaf is used, soak in hot water for about 10 minutes, squeeze, rinse, and set aside. Blend onion, leeks, green onions, parsley, basil, cilantro, ginger, and garlic and set aside. Add akanwu or nihkiy to the ugu (okongobong) leaves and boil for 20 minutes. Rinse properly and set aside. Cut beef into bite sizes, add to saucepan, add salt, and bring to a boil. In a larger saucepan, add 2 cups palm oil and heat for about 2 minutes. Do not bleach. Pour in ground crayfish and stir. Add blended herbs into the saucepan plus stock fish and pre-steamed beef. Continue to stir for 10 minutes; add 4 cups water and let cook for 30 minutes. Stock is not needed for this dish, so add water just as needed to cook the meats. Add salt, Maggi or Bouillon or Knorr cubes to taste. Add 2 teaspoons MammyDoro Meat Seasoning. Rinse and chop baby spinach and add to pot. Cook for 20 minutes. Rinse and squeeze ugu leaves and ukazi (eru) leaf into the saucepan. Mix properly, reduce the heat, and let simmer for about 20 minutes or until water dries off. Taste and adjust seasonings as needed.

Suggested Serving: Serve with eba(garri) pounded yam, rice, corn or oatmeal fufu.

INGREDIENTS

FINAL DISH

ERU

(Ukazi Sauce) - Serves 8

6 cups soaked and squeezed eru (ukazi)
1 lb. smoked turkey (optional)
10 bony smoked fish
4 cups palm oil
Salt, Maggi, Bouillon, or Knorr cubes
½ cup chopped ginger
2 cups chopped leeks
2 lbs. beef
1 lb. cow feet (optional)
1 lb. tripe (optional)
4 lbs. spinach (preferably fresh)
6 oz. stock fish bits
1 cup chopped onions
2 cups crayfish

Blend ginger, onions, leeks, and put aside. If eru is dried, boil water, soak eru in it for 30 minutes, rinse and squeeze. If fresh eru is used, rinse and squeeze. Cut meat into bite sizes, wash, and put into saucepan. If cow feet and tripe are used, boil them in advance and set aside. Add shredded smoked fish into meat. Add smoked turkey and blended herbs into meat. Add salt, Maggi, Bouillon, or Knorr cubes and pepper; cook for about 45 minutes. When meat is cooked, reduce the stock and keep in a bowl. Add chopped fresh spinach to the meat and stir until spinach is cooked. Take out the boiled pepper and put aside unless you want the eru spicy.

DO NOT COVER THE POT

Add eru gradually into spinach and mix; reduce the heat while doing this for about 5 minutes. Open up a hole in the center of the eru and pour in 2 cups palm oil. Let boil for 10 minutes. When oil is cooked, add ground crayfish to the oil and let it cook for about 5 minutes. Mix thoroughly, add pre-cooked cow feet and tripe and let simmer for 10 minutes. If too dry, add reserved stock bit by bit, watching consistency. Taste and adjust seasoningsste.

Suggested Serving: Serve with fufu of choice.

KALE SAUCE

(Bitter leaf alternative) - Serves 8

1 lb. cut kale (fresh or frozen)
1 lb. spinach (fresh or frozen)
2 cups peeled raw groundnuts and 8 cups water
1 cup of ground crayfish
2 cups chopped onion
1 cup chopped leeks
½ cup chopped garlic
1 cup chopped ginger
1 cup chopped basil, parsley and cilantro
3 lbs. beef, smoked turkey, hen, or mixed meats
1 lb. stock fish (optional)
2 cups vegetable oil
Salt, Maggi, Bouillon, or Knorr cubes to taste

Wash and blend kale with several cups water. Strain, squeeze, and put the juice in a large mug. Set aside. This can be used to make a healthy kale juice. Mix kale with finely chopped spinach. Spinach helps it to cook faster. Kale is a little rougher than the other greens but more nutritious. In a small pot add 6 cups water. Add raw peeled peanuts and ½ teaspoon of salt. Cook for 45 minutes or until well done. Blend ginger, garlic, leeks, onions, basil, parsley, and cilantro into a fine paste. Marinate and cook meat of choice adding ½ ground herbs to the meat with enough water to cook the meat. When groundnuts are done, blend into paste using its stock and a little more water if needed.

Pour vegetable oil into saucepan and heat for 1 minute. Add blended crayfish into heated oil and stir. Pour remaining ground herbs into crayfish and stir for about 20 minutes. Add peanut paste into the herbs and stir for about 20 minutes. Add the kale and spinach into the peanut, stirring slowly and watching consistency. "Ndole" is a sauce; mixture should not be too thick. It should look like a spinach dip. Keep stirring for about 15 minutes; add stock from the pre-cooked meat and 4 cups water. Cook for about 45 minutes, mixing every 10 minutes to prevent sticking. When kale is done, add the pre-cooked meat and let simmer for another 10 minutes.

Add ½ cup vegetable oil to saucepan, heat, and stir in the other cup of chopped onions. Let fry for 5 minutes and pour into the sauce (optional).

Suggested Serving: Serve with: Fried plantain, Steamed rice, Fufu of choice, boiled plantain, cassava, yam.

INGREDIENTS

FINAL DISH

A BOOK OF RECIPES, NUTRITIONAL INFORMATION & EDUCATION

NDOLE

(Bitter leaf sauce) - Serves 8

2 cups peeled raw groundnuts and 8 cups water
1 cup of ground crayfish
1 large onion
1 cup chopped leeks
½ cup chopped garlic
1 cup chopped ginger
1 cup vegetable oil
1 cup chopped basil, parsley, and cilantro
Beef, smoked turkey, hen, stock fish, or any meat of choice
Maggi, Bouillon, Knorr cubes, and sea salt to taste
Bitter leaf as needed

Cook bitter leaf until tender. If dry bitter leaf is used, add kanwa or baking soda to soften. Mix pre-cooked bitter leaf and spinach in ratio of 2:1 Bitter leaf to Spinach. Pre-cook raw peeled peanuts with water and salt until very tender and blend into paste using the stock from the cooked peanuts. Blend ginger, garlic, leeks, onions, basil, and parsley into a fine paste. Marinate and cook meat of choice adding half of the ground mixture of herbs with enough water. Put ½ of the ground herbs aside. Pre-heat cooking oil and add blended crayfish into heated oil and stir. Pour remaining ground herbs into crayfish and stir for 15 minutes. Add peanut paste into the herbs and stir for about 30 minutes. Add the bitter leaf and spinach into the peanut, stirring slowly and watching consistency. "Ndole" is a sauce, hence the mixture should not be thick; it should look like a spinach dip in consistency. You do not have to use all the pre-cooked bitter leaf. The quantity of bitter leaf used is a function of the peanut sauce. Add stock from your meat until desired consistency is reached and reduce the heat to low. Cook for 30 minutes. Add the meat and cook for another 10 minutes; reduce heat and let simmer until bitter leaf is well done.

Suggested Serving: Serve with fried plantains, miyondo, steamed rice, boiled plantains, boiled yams, fufu of choice.

INGREDIENTS

FINAL DISH

POTATO GREENS

(Sweet Potato Leaf sauce) - Serves 10   #themotherlandcookbook

6 bundles fresh potato greens
2 lbs. chicken and beef
1 cup chopped onions
1 teaspoon baking soda
½ cup chopped ginger
1 or 2 habanero peppers (optional)
½ cup of crayfish (optional)
2 teaspoons MammyDoro Meat Seasoning
1 cup mixed chopped basil, parsley, and cilantro
Salt, Maggi, or Knorr cubes to taste
1 lb. raw, deveined shrimp
1 lb. smoked turkey
2 cups chopped leeks
1 cup of pam oil
½ cup garlic
5 bony dry fish

Blend ginger, garlic, onions, leeks, basil, cilantro, parsley, and set aside. Soak bony fish in a bowl. Cut the potato leaves from the stems and place in a large bowl. When done cutting all the leaves, run water over them, rinsing a leaf at a time to remove any debris from the leaves. Finely slice the leaves and place in another bowl. Add 1 teaspoon of baking soda. Rub the sliced leaves between your palms, rinse, squeeze any excess water, and set aside. Take the skin off the chicken, cut into bite sizes, and set aside. Cut meat into bite sizes, rinse, and set aside. Cut the turkey as well and add to chicken. Rinse the meats and put into a saucepan. Add ¾ of the blended herbs, 1 teaspoon of salt, and 2 Maggi or Knorr cubes. Cook for 20 minutes. Add chicken and turkey and continue to cook for another 30 minutes. Do not add any water. Let the meats cook in their own juice. Blend crayfish and bony fish and set aside. Heat up 1 cup of palm oil in a large cooking pot on medium to high for 3 minutes. Add ground crayfish and bony fish and stir. Add the remaining blended herbs and continue to stir for about 5 minutes. Add potato greens and fry for 25 minutes, stirring frequently. Reduce heat to medium-low. Add pre-cooked meats and shrimp and let simmer for about 15 minutes or until water dries off.

Suggested Serving: Serve with rice, boiled potatoes, plantains or yams.

STEWED CABBAGE

Serves 8

3 lbs. cabbage
6 roma (plum) tomatoes
1 cup mixed chopped spring onions
¼ cup fresh thyme
1 cup chopped leeks
1 cup chopped onions
½ bell peppers (red, yellow, green)
½ teaspoon white pepper
1 cup vegetable oil (preferably olive oil)
2 teaspoons MammyDoro Vegetable Seasoning
Salt, Maggi, Knorr, or Bouillon cubes to taste

Chop cabbage into thin pieces as desired. Bring a pot of water to a boil, enough to soak the chopped cabbage. Add a little salt to boiling water and dump sliced cabbage into pot. Cover container to keep the heat in. Let boil for 5 minutes, remove cabbage, and dump in cold water. Strain and squeeze water from cabbage. Heat vegetable oil in sauce pan. Add chopped onions and stir for 5 minutes or until onion is translucent. Add blended leeks and spring onions and stir for 15 minutes. Add chopped tomatoes and stir for 15 minutes. Add salt and Maggi, Bouillon, or Knorr cubes to taste. Add 2 teaspoons of MammyDoro Greens Seasoning. Add sliced bell peppers and stir. Reduce heat to low and keep stirring until cooked and water dries out. Squeeze cabbage properly and add to the sauce. Pour water into sink—be careful not to spill it, as cabbage stock can be very pungent. Stir and let simmer for about 10 minutes. Continue to stir until vegetables are cooked to desired softness and water is dried up.

Suggested Serving: Serve with Plantains, Yams, Potatoes, or Steamed rice.

INGREDIENTS

FINAL DISH

A BOOK OF RECIPES, NUTRITIONAL INFORMATION & EDUCATION

SPINACH STEW

(Efo Riro – Minced meat, chicken or turkey) - Serves 8   #themotherlandcookbook

1lb turkey or chicken
4 lbs. spinach (frozen or fresh)
6 roma tomatoes
½ cup chopped garlic
½ cup chopped ginger
1 cups mixed chopped parsley, basil, and cilantro
1 cup chopped onion
1 cup chopped leeks
1 cup palm oil (or olive oil)
1 habanero pepper (optional)
MammyDoro Chicken or Meat Seasoning
Salt, Maggi or Knorr cubes & pepper to taste

Blend leeks, garlic, ginger, parsley, basil, and cilantro and set aside. Chop onions and tomatoes and set aside. Put meat of choice into a mixing bowl. Add ½ teaspoon salt and 2 Maggi or Knorr cubes or 1 Bouillon cube to the meat. Mix properly in the bowl before putting into a saucepan. Pour in blended herbs and begin to mix and stir on medium to low heat. DONOT add any oil at this time.   Stir for 10 minutes and add two cups of water or as needed and cook for twenty minutes. In another saucepan, add 1 cup of olive or palm oil and heat for about 1 or 2 minutes if palm oil is used. Add onions and stir until onions are translucent. Add tomatoes and a pinch of salt and continue to cook for 10 minutes. Pour the sauce into the meat and add 2 teaspoons of MammyDoro Vegetable Seasoning and continue to cook for another 10 minutes. Add spinach, mix properly to ensure an even distribution of meat and spinach. Add a cup or two of warm water if mixture is too dry. Let simmer for 10 minutes. Then turn off the stove. Leave saucepan on stove for 5 minutes, taste and adjust seasonings and serve.

Suggested Serving: Serve with steamed rice, boiled potatoes, yams, plantain or cassava or fufu of choice.

INGREDIENTS

FINAL DISH

MISCELLANEOUS

KANWA/AKANWU

Akanwu (Igbo name) or Kanwa (Hausa name) is a naturally occurring bicarbonate that has various uses. This naturally occurring mineral has different varieties but have similar properties. They are all alkaline and soapy when dissolved in water. Their culinary use is as a tenderizer, preserver, and emulsifying agent. Beef stock and palm oil will normally not mix together. But when the akanwu liquid is added to it and blended, it becomes a thick, yellow soup ready to be eaten with Achu fufu or as an appetizer, if made with cow feet (nkwobi) or goat head (isi ewu). Akanwu is used as a thickener in Achu soup or Isiewu. Akanwu is also used as a food color enhancer. When added to greens while boiling, the color is preserved and made even brighter. It is believed to remove the gas in beans that would otherwise cause bloating. But there is a possibility of Akanwu/kanwa containing impurities and debris, such as sand, clay, metals, and other minerals, even lead. A better alternative is the pearl ash liquid, which is made from burnt wood or plant ashes, like the peelings of plantains.

Brew your own akanwu/ kanwa (nihkiy) by preserving plantain peelings and adding them to your BBQ grill to provide the ash that contains even better nutrients than the naturally occurring mineral. The ash from burnt plantain peelings contains potassium, calcium, iron, and magnesium. Use your coffee maker and instead of coffee, add the ash and brew. If you do not have a coffee maker, simply put the ash into a perforated can, add water, mix, and let the mineral water drip. This is a very safe alternative to solid akanwu/kanwa because it is free of lead contamination. If you must use akanwu, then boil it, sieve using a cheese cloth, pour into bottles, and preserve for future use.

BEEF PATTI FILLING

1 lb. ground beef
1 cup chopped green bell peppers
1 cup chopped onions
½ cup chopped ginger & garlic
1 cup chopped celery sticks
2 Maggi, Knorr cubes or 1 Bouillon cube
1 flat teaspoon salt
½ habanero pepper (optional)
1 cup chopped carrots
2 cups chopped or grated potatoes (sweet or Irish)
2 teaspoons MammyDoro Meat Seasoning

Blend the ginger, garlic, celery, parsley, cilantro, basil, and pepper with ½ cup water. In a non-stick pot, add minced meat, salt, Maggi, Bouillon, or Knorr. Add MammyDoro Meat Seasoning and stir properly. Add blended herbs and stir for about 15 minutes. Then add chopped onions, chopped potatoes, and celery to the meat. Cook for another 10 minutes. In another pot, boil peas and carrots for 10 minutes. Strain and add to the meat. Add chopped bell peppers and curry and cook for about 5 minutes. Add 1 cup of water, lower the heat, and let simmer. Taste and adjust seasonings.
Ground beef is greasy, so let the meat cook in its own fat. This will help to reduce the oiliness of the filling.

Suggested Serving: Add to the dough as desired and bake.

INGREDIENTS

FINAL DISH

CHICKEN/TURKEY PATTI FILLING

1 lb. ground turkey or chicken
2 cups chopped potatoes
1 cup chopped green bell peppers
1 cup chopped onions
1 cup chopped celery sticks
2 Maggi cubes or Knorr
1 flat teaspoon sea salt
½ cup vegetable oil
½ habanero pepper (optional)
1 cup chopped carrots
1 cup bread crumbs
1 teaspoon Mammy Doro Chicken Seasoning

Blend the celery, onions, and pepper with ½ cup of water. Heat up oil in saucepan. Add blended mixture and stir. Add salt and Maggi, Bouillon, or Knorr and cook for about 10 minutes. Add minced chicken or turkey and chicken seasoning into sauce. Stir and cook for 15 minutes. Add bell peppers and cook for about 5 minutes. Lower the heat and let simmer.

In another pot, boil chopped potatoes and carrots. When done, strain and add to the sauce. Mix properly. Let cool, add bread crumps, and mix.

Suggested Serving: Add to the dough as desired and bake.

INGREDIENTS

FINAL DISH

A BOOK OF RECIPES, NUTRITIONAL INFORMATION & EDUCATION

FISH PATTI FILLING

1 lb. fish fillet of choice
2 cups chopped potatoes
1 cup chopped green bell peppers
1 cup chopped onions
1 cup chopped celery sticks
2 Maggi, Knorr cubes or 1 Bouillon cube
1 flat teaspoon sea salt
½ cup vegetable oil
½ habanero pepper (optional)
1 teaspoon of curry
1 cup chopped carrots
1 cup of bread crumps
2 teaspoons MammyDoro Seafood Seasoning

Cut fish in small slices and add to bowl. Add seafood seasoning, salt, and put on the side. Blend the celery, onions, and pepper with ½ cup of water. Heat up oil in saucepan for 1 minute. Add blended mixture and stir. Add salt and Maggi, Bouillon, or Knorr and cook for about 10 minutes. Add fish, curry, and bell peppers. Lower the heat and let simmer. In another pot, boil chopped potatoes and carrots. When done, strain and add to the sauce. Mix properly until fish becomes mashed.

In another pot, boil chopped potatoes and carrots. When done, strain and add to the fish. Mix properly. Let cool, add bread crumbs, and mix.

Suggested Serving: Add to the dough as desired and bake

INGREDIENTS

FINAL DISH

FERMENTED FOODS

Fermented foods are a real sticking point for many people. Although they may not taste and smell good, due to the fermentation process of the foods, they are actually very beneficial to the digestive system. It takes an acquired taste to appreciate these foods, but once you try them, your taste buds begin to appreciate them. In the Western world, fermentation is a simple, safe, and effective way of food preservation whose origin dates back into history. In Africa traditionally fermented foods are slowly moving away from the mostly primitive stages and cottage industry to more industrialized forms, as seen in the production and exportation of fermented cassava and corn products from West African countries.

According to Dr. David Williams, a Medical Researcher, Biochemist, and Chiropractor, traditionally fermented foods have many benefits to the digestive system. These foods protect the stomach and intestinal lining when the stomach produces too much acid. When hydrochloric acid production in the stomach is low, fermented foods help increase the acidity of gastric juices. As we age, production of digestive juices and enzymes needed to break down the food decreases. It is therefore recommended to eat traditionally fermented foods regularly, especially those with diabetes, as carbohydrates in lactic acid fermented foods have already been broken down and do not place any extra burden on the pancreas.

Some example of main dishes are Ghana's Banku (fermented corn & cassava), Ghana's kenkey (fermented corn), Ivory Coast's Attieke, Cameroon's Miyondo, Shindodo, Bobolo, kumkum, gari (fermented cassava), Ethiopia's Injera (fermented teff), Edamame, and South Africa's Miso Soup, which is made from fermented soybeans and rice or barley.

Back in the '60s and '70s, when there were no processed food flavor enhancers, such as Maggi, Knorr, or Bouillon, Cameroonians and Nigerians used fermented legumes to enhance the flavor of their foods. Though pungent in aroma, Dawadawa (iru), prepared from the seeds of African locust beans in Nigeria, was a must have for soups. Today, some people still use this flavor enhancer. It is terrible that the production of this seasoning has been reduced and the price has gone up so much. Maggi, Knorr, and Bouillon cubes are more common in African cuisines today. If the production of dawadawa was improved and refined, more people, knowing the benefits of fermented foods, would be likely to buy this item instead of Maggi, Knorr, or Bouillon cubes.

Before the advent of beer factories in Africa, alcoholic beverages were made from various grains. Some examples are Cameroon's Kwacha, kimbusha, Shah, Corn beer, kaffir beer; South Africa's Sorghum Beer; North Nigeria's Burukutu and Pito made from sorghum, corn and or millet; Sudan's sorghum fermented beverage, Merissa; and Northern Togo's tchapalo from white fonio.

Up until today, all African breakfast porridges were made from one kind of fermented grain or another. Grains are severely damaged in the commercial making of breakfast cereals. Eating them in their natural form is more beneficial, and fermentation preserves all the nutrients and vitamins. As an example, African breakfast porridges from fermented grains are Nigeria's ogi, akamu, or pap; Senegal's millet, lakh, or fonde; and Tanzania's uji, just to name a few.

Fulani cattle breeders depend on the production and sale of milk for immediate revenue while the cattle are sold later on. Unable to afford refrigeration, milk fermentation has been an age-old practice. Fermented milk is also greatly consumed on the continent, especially by Moslem populations who depend on a lot of porridge dishes during prayer and fasting periods. Senegal's Lakh, or fonde, is accompanied by fermented milk. East and South African Amasi, fermented milk, used in eating pap, is a source of lactobacilli needed to synthesize vitamin K.

The consumption of traditionally fermented milk in some African countries is affected by the perceived poor methods of processing, lack of investment in this industry, and lack of sensitization on the benefits of fermented milk—all to the detriment of the health of the population.

It is safer to eat fermented foods than a bowl of salad. Studies have shown that food borne bacteria like E. coli can be eliminated by the practice of fermenting foods. Fermented foods are full of bacteria that help with digestion of food and provide much needed bacteria in the gut.

SOME TRADITIONALLY FERMENTED FOODS

Miyondo - Bobolo

Water Fufu

Kenkey

Gari

Dawadawa Seasoning

Cassava Flour-Kum Kum

INJERA

Injera is a sourdough-risen unleavened flatbread with a unique, slightly spongy texture. It is made from teff flour and it is the national dish of Ethiopia and Eritrea. A similar variant is eaten in Somalia, Djibouti, Yemen, and Sudan. This bread is yeast-free and gluten-free which makes it a good alternative to regular wheat bread, which is made from flour and contains gluten. The good news is that you do not have to make injera. You can simply buy it from the Ethiopian, Eritrean or Somali food stores around the country. All you need to do is prepare the accompaniments for injera. There is a wide range to choose from; stewed lentils, salads, stewed lamb or beef, chick-peas, split peas and greens. You will find these recipes in this book.

ATTIEKE

Attiéké is a product of cassava (yuca), and it is an Ivorian staple. It is a popular dish in restaurants in urban cities in Ivory Coast. It is typically served with stewed onions and tomatoes and either BBQ fish or chicken in restaurants. In the coastal rural areas, attiéké is served with fish and palm butter stew (mbanga soup—sauce graine). It is quicker and more cost effective to serve attiéké in restaurants with inexpensive sides.

Attiéké has the look and feel of garri (eba) or couscous, but it is processed differently from how garri is processed in Nigeria, Ghana, and Cameroon. The cooking method of the dried attiéké is very similar to couscous. Attiéké also comes frozen, and most people would prefer the frozen one to the dried one. It is not a wheat product, so it is a good example of a gluten-free food to eat. It is typically served with grilled fish, chicken, and a mixture of tomatoes and onions but could also be served with stewed meats, poultry, fish, and vegetables. The acidity from the tomato stew neutralizes the sour flavor of attiéké and gives it a very savory taste. The sourness is a result of the fermentation of the cassava in processing attiéké. First, it is an acquired taste to appreciate the food, but once you get used to it, you would crave for the grain always. It is also very affordable. You can find it in local African food stores in your neighborhood.

Cook the dry attiéké the same way you would do your Moroccan couscous. Mix equal parts of water and attiéké in a bowl and set aside for 10 minutes. The attiéké will absorb water and swell up. Wrap the bowl with plastic wrap and cook in the microwave for 2-3 minutes per cup of attiéké or use a steam pot and cheesecloth. With the frozen attiéké, you just need to defrost and use a fork to spread it out; it is ready to be served.

INGREDIENTS

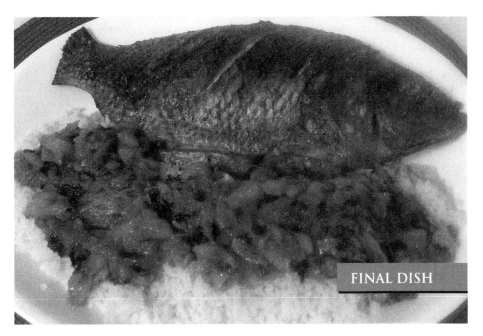

FINAL DISH

KEKAH

In the early '40s, when people were going to war, their families would prepare a dish made from corn and peanuts for them to take along. This dish was and is still very filling. It is also a very balanced meal. No seasoning was necessary, except the addition of a pinch of salt to wake up the natural flavor in the peanut and corn. The corn and peanut were fried, ground, and mixed together and steam cooked. The frying was a method of preservation, as it would remove the water from the grains. It was also assumed that it added flavor to the dish instead of grinding and mixing raw corn and peanuts. Kekah was a food for survival back then, but today it is a delicacy in the villages, as it is no longer a common food item in towns and cities. The fast pace of activities in the cities lends itself more to kimbur than kekah. In the '60s and '70s, parents used to make kekah for their kids who went to boarding school. It would last for a good 3-4 months without spoiling. Kekah is similar to Nigerian Kokoro because both food items are made from corn and peanuts, but Kekah is markedly different from Kokoro because it is made from equal amounts of corn and peanuts to balance the protein that is missing in corn. Kokoro is basically corn with a little bit of peanuts. Kekah is steam-cooked, but kokoro is deep fried. Kokoro is still a very popular snack in Nigeria. It would be helpful to improve on the consistency by increasing the peanut content.Nowadays, the West provides compounded corn and peanut bars for kids in hunger-stricken areas. This had been a tradition in Africa for decades. This is a good alternative to unhealthy snacks. It is usually wrapped in banana or plantain leaves but could also be cooked in aluminum foil or both. Steam for 45 minutes; serve or preserve. I have improvised with cornmeal and roasted unsalted peanuts. Simple grind peanuts using dry grinder, add corn, salt, sugar and black pepper. Mix and steam cook.

1 cup of corn meal
3 cups of water
½ teaspoon salt
2 cup of peanuts

1 teaspoon freshly ground black pepper
1 tablespoon brown sugar

PREPPING

Prepping is key to any delicious dish. This is mostly done in restaurants not because of the need to serve food in a timely fashion in order to impress and retain customers but to enhance the taste of our foods, to minimize waste, and to making cooking easy and fun. We can use some family time with our younger kids to prep for the ingredients that we use often in cooking. We can prep the meats that we use also so that when it comes cooking time, most of the hard part is already taken care of. Remember that herbs provide flavor in foods that, if properly seasoned, we do not need a lot of salt, monosodium glutamate (MSG), Knorr, Bouillon, or Maggi cubes to enhance the tastes of our foods. You will notice that most of my recipes use garlic, ginger, basil, parsley, cilantro, onions, and leeks. To me, leeks is a must have in the kitchen. This is the one ingredient that my mother made sure we had in the kitchen all the time. It is noteworthy that herbs are highly perishable, so we must come up with ways of preserving them for our daily cooking. My suggestion is that you should encourage your teenage kids to prep these herbs and store them in the freezer and enough in the refrigerator to last a week, at most two weeks. Kids enjoy helping in the kitchen if only we let them. They can wash and chop up the herbs and then blend, pour in storage containers, and label them. An example of a good way to prep these herbs and store would be to make containers for the following:

1. Leeks & green onions
2. Garlic & ginger
3. Onions
4. Basil, parsley & cilantro

Then add vegetable oil to about 2" from the top of the bottle and store. When you need to cook, simply scoop how much you need and you are good to go. For your meats, take the skin off your chicken or turkey, cut them into desired sizes, add a little salt and seasoning, and store in Ziploc bags in the freezer. Not only will cooking be easier and faster when you are ready but the meat will be so tasty because it has marinated properly. Wash your fish with lemon, lime, or vinegar. Add some salt and seasoning and store in the freezer.

Your fresh vegetables can also be parboiled, squeezed, and frozen. This is if you prefer buying fresh collards, turnips, and mustards. Otherwise, frozen vegetables are as good as the fresh ones. Just do not keep them for too long because they might get freezer burns and discoloration.

QUINOA PILAF

(Vegetarian) - Serves 8

1 lb. quinoa seeds
1 lb. cut carrots and peas
2 green onions
3 roma (plum) tomatoes
1 habanero pepper (optional)
1 cup black olives (optional)
1 cup chopped parsley, basil, cilantro
2 teaspoons MammyDoro Vegetable Seasoning
Salt, Maggi, Bouillon, or Knorr cubes to taste
½ teaspoon of baking soda
1 large onion
3 garlic cloves
1 teaspoon curry
5 tablespoons coconut oil

Blend garlic, parsley, basil, cilantro, and pepper (optional) using ½ cup of water and set aside. Add 8 cups water in a large pot and bring to a boil. Then add ½ teaspoon of salt and ½ teaspoon of baking soda. Add quinoa seeds and boil for 20 minutes. Strain using a sieve; quinoa seeds are very small. Open running water over the sieve and rinse to remove bitterness and set aside. The baking soda helps to remove the pungent smell and bitter taste from the quinoa seeds.

In another pot, add carrots, peas, 4 cups water, and a pinch of salt. Cook for 10 minutes, strain, and set aside. Put oil into saucepan and heat for 1 - 2 minutes. Add finely chopped onion, green onions, 2 Maggi or Knorr cubes, and a pinch of salt to the saucepan. Cook for 10 minutes, stirring every 5 minutes until onions soften. Add blended herbs and continue to stir for another 5 minutes. Add chopped tomatoes and stir for 5 minutes. Then add 3 cups water and let cook for 20 minutes, stirring every 5 minutes. Add finely chopped bell peppers, mix properly, and let cook for 5 minutes. Then add pre-boiled quinoa and mix. Add pre-cooked vegetables and chopped black olives (optional). Stir until water dries off. Turn off the heat. Taste and adjust seasonings. Let sit for 5 minutes and serve.

Suggested Serving: Serve hot with any meat of choice (grilled chicken or fish, steak or pan fried fish or chicken).

STIR FRIED GOAT OR LAMB

Serves 4

3 lbs. goat or lamb
½ cup vegetable oil
1 teaspoon MammyDoro Meat Seasoning
½ cup mixed chopped ginger and garlic
½ cup chopped onions
Pepper to taste
Sea salt, Maggi, Bouillon, or Knorr cubes to taste

Cut goat or lamb into bite sizes. Wash and put them in a pot. Add water and salt. Cook for about 20 minutes and strain—goat or lamb meat is a little gamey and greasy (this is why the meat should pre-boiled, to reduce the gaminess and the excess grease). Blend the ginger, garlic, onions, pepper, and put aside. Put vegetable oil in saucepan and heat for 2 minutes. Add goat meat, Maggi/Bouillon/Knorr cubes, and mix properly. Add MammyDoro Meat Seasoning and the blended herbs and continue to stir for about 5 minutes over medium heat. Add 4 cups water or enough to cook the meat. Cook for about 30 minutes or until meat is tender and water dries up.

This is similar to the Nigerian Asun dish, which is served with slices of onions, green bell peppers, tomatoes, and habanero peppers.

Suggested Serving: Serve with greens and fried plantain or as needed.

STIR FRIED HEN or TURKEY

Serves 4

3 lbs. hen or turkey
1 cup vegetable oil
1 teaspoon MammyDoro Meat Seasoning
½ cup mixed chopped ginger, onions, garlic
Sea salt, Maggi, Bouillon, or Knorr cubes to taste

Blend ginger, garlic, onions, and pepper and put aside. Cut hen or turkey into desired sizes. Put in a large pot and add water to cover the meat plus 1 teaspoon of salt. Cook for about 20 minutes and strain; hen or turkey meat is a little gamey. Put vegetable oil in saucepan and heat for 2 minutes. Add 1 teaspoon of salt, hen or turkey, 2 Maggi or Knorr cubes or 1 Bouillon cube, and mix properly. Add 2 teaspoons MammyDoro Meat Seasoning and the blended herbs. Continue to stir for about 10 minutes over high heat. Add 8 cups water or enough to cook the hen or turkey. Reduce the heat to medium. Cook for about 45 minutes or until hen or turkey is tender and water dries off.

Suggested Serving: Serve with greens and fried plantain or as needed.

STUFFED TOMATOES

Serves 6

6 slicing tomatoes
2 cans tuna (5 oz. each) or meat of choice
½ cup peas, ½ cup sweet corn, or 1 can mixed vegetables (15 oz.)
½ cup diced celery
½ cup chopped black olives
½ chopped bell peppers (green, red, yellow)
½ cup chopped carrots
Dressing of choice
Salt to taste
Freshly ground black pepper to taste

Wash tomatoes and dry them using a clean cloth. Slice top about an inch deep. Use teaspoon to scoop out flesh carefully without boring a hole in the tomatoes. Use a sharp knife to create a "V" shape decoration around the top where the cut is made on the tomato. Save the bits of tomatoes to include in salad. If canned peas and corn are used, open can, rinse properly, and put in large bowl. Clean and chop up carrots and add to bowl. Slice bell peppers, cube, and add to bowl. Open tuna or meat of choice and add to bowl. Add salt to taste, add dressing and mix properly, add freshly ground black pepper. Mix and fill up tomatoes.

Suggested Serving: Serve with bread of choice as an appetizer.

INGREDIENTS

FINAL DISH

VEGETABLE PATTI FILLING

Makes 20 patties

3 carrots
2 lbs. cabbage
1 cup finely chopped onions
4 roma (plum) tomatoes
1 habanero pepper (optional)
1 cup chopped parsley, cilantro, and basil
2 bell peppers finely chopped (any colors
1 cup finely chopped leeks or green onions
¼ cup chopped garlic
¼ cup chopped ginger
2 Maggi/Knorr cubes or 1 Bouillon cube to taste
2 teaspoons MammyDoro Vegetable Seasoning
Olive oil or coconut oil
2 celery sticks finely chopped
4 medium sweet potatoes
¼ cup fresh thyme
1 teaspoon salt or to taste

Chop or grate sweet potatoes and carrots and set aside. Chop or grate cabbage and set aside. Chop or grate tomatoes and onions and set aside. Bring water to a boil. Add cabbage and 1 teaspoon of salt. Cook for 5 minutes, strain, and dump in cold water. Blend ginger, garlic, leeks, or green onions, thyme, parsley, cilantro, basil, and pepper with 1 cup of water. Heat oil in sauce pan for 1 minute. Add chopped onions and stir. Add tomatoes, mix properly, and stir for 5 minutes. Add blended mixture and stir. Add 2 Maggi or Knorr cubes or 1 Bouillon cube and cook for about 20 minutes. Add chopped sweet potatoes, carrots, and bell peppers. Add 2 teaspoons MammyDoro Vegetable Seasoning and 1 cup of water. Cook for about 10 minutes. Squeeze pre-cooked cabbage, add to sauce pan, and mix properly. Taste and adjust seasonings. Lower the heat and let simmer for about 15 minutes. Take pot off the stove. Let cool and use as desired.

Suggested Serving: Use as filling for vegetable Patties. Could also be served with steamed rice.

INGREDIENTS

FINAL DISH

VEGGIE OMELET

Serves 5

6 brown eggs
2 roma (plum) tomatoes
½ cup chopped onions
½ cup chopped leeks or green onions
½ cup chopped celery (leaves only)
½ bell peppers (red & green)
1 teaspoon MammyDoro Vegetable Seasoning
1 Maggi or Knorr cube or ½ Bouillon cube
½ cup olive oil
1 habanero pepper (optional)
1 teaspoon salt or to taste
6 oz. baby spinach
1 teaspoon curry

Chop up the tomatoes, onions, leeks, bell peppers, habanero pepper, and spinach and set aside. Add ½ cup olive oil into a large, non-stick pot. Heat the oil for 1 minute and add onions and leeks. Stir for 2 minutes and add chopped tomatoes. Add salt and Maggi, Knorr, or ½ Bouillon cube and continue to stir for 5 minutes. Add chopped celery and let cook for 10 minutes. Add bell peppers and habanero peppers and stir for 5 minutes. Add curry and MammyDoro Vegetable Seasoning and stir. Beat eggs properly with a hand mixer and pour into sauce. Reduce the heat and mix continuously for 5 minutes. Add chopped spinach and mix for another minute. Pour the eggs into a large bowl and serve.

Suggested Serving: Serve with fried plantains, fried sweet potatoes, toasted potatoes or rice puff puff.

INGREDIENTS

FINAL DISH

TOASTED POTATOES

Serves 1

1 potato (sweet or Irish)
A pinch of salt
A pinch of MammyDoro Vegetable Seasoning
Frying oil

Place the potato (sweet or Irish) length-wise and cut into ½-inch chunks. Peel, wash, and put in a small pot. Add a pinch of salt and a pinch of MammyDoro Vegetable Seasoning. Add 1 cup of water to the potato and put on the stove. Bring to a boil and let cook for 5 minutes. Strain and put on the side. Heat the frying oil for about 5 minutes. Put in potato and fry for 5 minutes until golden brown, especially on the edges. Use a fork to check whether the inside is properly cooked. Remove and place on a paper towel. This method makes the potato crisp on the outside and nicely cooked on the inside. Steaming the potatoes before frying seals the potatoes from absorbing excess frying oil.

Suggested Serving: Serve with veggie omelet, stewed greens or any stew of choice.

BBQ & GRILLING

It is generally believed that BBQ as a method of cooking was brought to America by the African slaves. It is most commonly done in the south, especially in South Carolina, Tennessee, Oklahoma, Kansas, and Texas. Each state has its own peculiarities, especially in the meat cut, the wood used, and the sauces as well.

While there is a vast degree of variation and overlap in terminology and method surrounding this form of cooking, the generally accepted difference between barbecue and grilling is in the cooking time and type of heat used: grilling is generally done "hot and fast" over direct heat from low-smoke fuels (with the flame contacting the meat itself), while barbecuing is usually done "low and slow" over indirect heat from high-smoke fuels (with the flame not contacting the meat directly).

BBQ is common and most prevalent among Muslims in various African countries. It is very common to find local grills on road junctions, in front of drinking spots, and in restaurants. Traditionally, Muslims prefer lamb, chicken and beef, and tendons, while others, mostly Christians, may prefer fish and chicken. In Eastern Africa, lamb, goat, and beef are most common, and Kenyans use "Nyamchoma," which is BBQ goat meat or lamb, as a side for their fufu (ugali). BBQ fish is a specialty of Cameroon, and it is not uncommon to run into a stranger in the West who craves for Cameroonian BBQ fish. This is typically found along the road side near drinking spots and along the beaches of Limbe and Kribi. Kankan (hot suya spice) is used mostly in Cameroon and Northern Nigeria to eat the BBQ meat (suya). It is believed that this spice also has medicinal properties.

Chicken is grilled in parts of the Northern Region of Cameroon as a prep method for Kahti Kahti, a delicious sauce eaten with greens and corn fufu. The flame causes a darkening to the meat while producing a nice smoke aroma in the final dish.

Peanut is used in seasoning blends to enhance the flavor of meat and act as a tenderizer as well. This is commonly used in Nigeria and Cameroon. It is better to use natural tenderizers for your BBQ meat. Tenderizers enhance the flavor of meat, break down protein, and make chewing easier. Pineapple, kiwis, and papaya contain vegetable enzymes that dissolve protein and connective tissues. You can blend any of these fruits and pour over meat. This process can be done in merely a few hours and works best on thin cuts. Salt is a tenderizer and a flavor enhancer—use Kosher or natural sea salt. Ginger is an herb that gives great flavor to your meat, also acting as a tenderizer because it contains proteolytic enzymes which naturally break down proteins.

NORTHERN & SAHARAN AFRICA CUISINES

Algeria, like the other Maghreb countries of North West Africa, eat couscous and lamb as well as Mediterranean fish. Spices like ginger, fennel, mace, anise, cumin, black pepper, and chilies are popular in Algerian cuisine. Chakhchoukha, a stew (marqa), is made from diced lamb, tomatoes, onions, chickpeas, zucchini, carrots, and green peppers. This stew is served over couscous. The traditional Amazigh—flatbread made from semolina flour—is eaten with every meal. Algerian meat of choice is Merguez, a spicy lamb sausage. Chickpeas are often part of Algerian stews, and beetroot and anchovies are commonly used as well. Algerian cuisine is highly influenced by the French, Spanish, and Turkish cuisines. The Nile perch, found in Lake Chad, together with tilapia are the main source of protein for the people of Chad. Millet, sorghum, and rice are eaten with sauces often prepared with cassava leaf and okra. Tomato stews containing goat meat are also part of Chadian cuisine.

The national dish of Egypt is Kushari, a dish made by combining pasta, tomato sauce, lentils, onions, chickpeas, and rice. These food items were brought from other countries to Egypt, but Egyptians came up with the delicious vegetarian mix called Kushari. Fatta is eaten during special events, such as the birth of the first child and in religious celebrations amongst Christian and Moslem alike. It is a very high-calorie dish made of rice, deep fried bread, poached eggs, and large chunks of stewed beef. Mulukhiya (jute leaf) soup is also part of Egyptian cuisine. The leaves are finely chopped and cooked in the broth of chicken, beef, or rabbit. Some variations are made with fish and shrimp broth, mostly in Alexandria and Port Said. Ingredients like garlic and coriander are also used to make Mulukhiya.

Jute leaves are also used in making sauces in Cameroon (keleng Keleng or kren kren), in Nigeria (Ewudu), and in Liberia (palaver sauce). The difference between these sauces and Mulukhiya is that meat, smoked fish, crayfish, crawfish, shrimp, and palm oil are included in the sauce in Cameroon, Liberia, and Nigeria, instead of just cooking the jute leaves in the broth. In West Africa, it is believed that the slipperiness of the sauce makes for easy swallowing of the fufu, since fufu is not chewed. Only the meat is chewed.

Falafel is a popular snack in Egypt made primarily from fava beans. Some variations of this dish are made with a combination of fava and garbanzo beans. It is similar to black-eyed peas fritters (akara) in West Africa but more flavorful than Akara beans. Falafel is made with lots of seasonings; i.e., cumin, coriander, and herbs like parsley, cilantro, and above all garlic.

Libyan diet is rich in seafood and like the other Maghreb nations, couscous is a specialty. Virgin olive oil is mostly used in cooking due to its great taste and its anti-inflammatory properties. Palm dates are also a major ingredient in Libyan cuisine. They are used in making magrood—a dough that is made by mixing Semolina flour, wheat flour, olive oil, and dates. A typical Libyan stew is made from meat, potatoes, chickpeas, and tomato sauce. This recipe is common in all of the North African Maghreb nations. The stew is typically served over steamed rice or couscous.

Lebrak is a Libyan dish made from stuffing vine leaves locally called esselk leaves. The leaves are stuffed with a mixture made from rice, tomato puree, herbs and spices, garlic, parsley, scallions, and pieces of meat or minced meat. You can find pre-bottled vine leaves in brine, but you must wash them thoroughly to remove the excess salt from the leaves before using them to cook Lebrak. Any other green leaf can do the job as well. Utshu or Bazin is a form of fufu made from barley flour. The barley is roasted, ground, sifted, and stored for use when needed. This flour is therefore pre-processed, hence the cooking of Bazin takes just a few minutes. The barley flour can be substituted with organic wheat or rice flour. The cooking should take a little longer because these flours are somewhat raw. Bazin is prepared by boiling water, putting part of it aside, and stirring in the flour while mixing until the dough is stiff. This is the same way "eba" or "gari" is made.

The stew used to eat Bazin is made using lamb, chicken, or fish together with garlic, turmeric, tomato, and paprika (mild or hot). The prepared Bazin is placed on a plate and the sauce poured over it with pieces of meat or fish placed around the lump of Bazin. Libyans use their hands to tear off the Bazin and dip in the sauce before eating, just like West, Central, East, and South Africans eat fufu from yam, cassava, oatmeal, rice, plantain, or corn. Mali's population is concentrated in the south west of the country, hence the influence of Senegalese dishes in Malian cuisine. Rice, millet, sorghum, and folio are eaten in Mali as well as Senegal. The typical Senegalese style peanut sauce (mahfe) ccoked with fish, meat, and vegetables is prepared and eaten with fufu from yam or plantain. It is also served over steamed rice. The fish in Mali is from the Niger River, since the country is landlocked. Foutou banane (plantain fufu) and foutou igname (yam fufu) are eaten with Tigadeguena, which is similar to the Senegalese mahfe (peanut sauce). Poulet Yassa (chicken onion stew) is also common in Malian cuisine, as it is in most of the neighboring countries of Senegal. The chicken is marinated with spices and a lot of lime juice, which acts as a tenderizer to the tough chicken that is common in this region. Malians also enjoy a breakfast porridge made from grains, which is similar to "akamu" in Nigeria or "pap" in Cameroon. In the latter countries, the porridge is made from corn.

Mauritania's cuisine is influenced by Senegalese and North Western African cuisine. Thiebou dienne is the national dish of Mauritania, and it is eaten daily. There are two types of this dish in Mauritania: white and pink Thiebou dienne. This is a rice dish that is made with fish, tomatoes, and vegetables like cassava, okra, cabbage, carrots, and eggplants. It is also the national dish of Senegal.

The onion stew (Yassa) is cooked with fried chicken but chicken being inexpensive, most people use meatballs to make Yassa in Senegal. Mahfe a typical Senegalese peanut sauce and is also eaten in Mauritania, cooked with goat or camel meat. Hakko, ground bean leaves (fresh wah in Cameroon), is cooked and served over couscous made from millet, wheat, or barley.

Like Algeria, Morocco's staple food is couscous served with chicken stew. The stew is made with Moroccan spice blends, tomatoes, and chickpeas. The stew differs from one region of Morocco to the other.

Nigeriens, like Malians, eat porridge from millet for breakfast. Rice is also eaten with different kinds of meats and stews. The fieriness of Nigerien food is believed to be as a result of the influence of Arabian travelers who also brought ginger, nutmeg, cinnamon, saffron, and cloves to Niger. Corn, cassava, sorghum, and beans are also eaten in Niger. Puff puff is a popular snack in Niger, and couscous is reserved for special occasions.

Tunisian foods are a combination of Arabic, French, Middle Eastern, and Mediterranean cuisines. Tunisian cuisine is mainly seafood or lamb cooked with tomatoes and spices. The fieriness of Tunisian food is due to the influence of Arabian and Turkish cuisines. Lablabi is a thick Tunisian soup made with chickpeas, cumin, and garlic. This soup is served over small pieces of crispy bread. Raw eggs or soft-cooked eggs are sometimes added to the soup. Herbs like cilantro, parsley, and scallions are also used in making Lablabi.

Western Saharan cuisine is mostly influenced by Moroccan cuisine. Fish is a source of protein for the people of Western Sahara. Meifrisa is the traditional dish of Western Sahara. This is a stew made from lamb or camel meat, onions, and garlic and is served over unleavened bread. Couscous and goat stew are also part of Western Saharan cuisine.

GLOSSARY

Akanwu/Kanwa/Potash

Crystallized hydrous carbonate of potassium used as a tenderizer, thickener of foods in Africa. Usually greyish-white in color and has a soapy feel when dissolved in water. It has been known to contain lead which is poisonous to the human body.

Dawadawa/Iru/ugba

A spice made from fermented African locust beans. Very commonly used in Nigerian cuisine as a good and healthy alternative to maggi or knorr or bouillon cubes.

Njangsa

Omega-3-Rich seed (Ricinodendron Heudelotii) used in most fish dishes in Tropical Africa. Also known as Bofeko, Djansang, Essang, Essessang, Ezezang, Kishongo, Munguella, Njasang, Okhuen.

Nihkiy

A liquid brewed from wood or plantain peeling ashes that is used in the same way as Akanwu. More nutritious and safe

SEASONINGS

Mammy Doro Fish/Shrimp Seafood Seasoning

Mammy Doro All Purpose Peppersoup Seasoning

Mammy Doro Chicken Seasoning

Mammy Doro Porridge "Ekwang" Seasoning

Mammy Doro Suya Seasoning

Mammy Doro Blackened Fish "Mbongo" Seasoning

SEASONINGS (CONTINUED)

Mammy Doro "Greens"
Seasoning

Mammy Doro "Meat"
Seasoning

Mammy Doro "Beans"
Seasoning

Mammy Doro Hot Scented
Seasoning

Mammy Doro Achu/Ishewu
Seasoning

Mammy Doro "Jollof Rice"
Seasoning

A BOOK OF RECIPES, NUTRITIONAL INFORMATION & EDUCATION

SEASONINGS (CONTINUED)

Mammy Doro "African
Blue Basil" Seasoning

Mammy Doro "Njangsa"
Seasoning

Buy your favorite seasoning blends at motherlandspices.com

CPSIA information can be obtained
at www.ICGtesting.com
Printed in the USA
FSOW04n1057140717
36145FS